The Last
SEA DOG

Making Waves

The real lives of sporting heroes on, in & under the water

Also in this series...

My Life In A Blue Suit
by Jim Saltonstall
The man who helped make Britain
great at sailing

In Bed With The Atlantic
by Kitiara Pascose
An anxious non-sailor's Atlantic circuit

A Wild Call
by Martyn Murray
One man's voyage in pursuit of freedom

Sailing Around Britain
by Kim C. Sturgess
A weekend sailor's voyage in 50 day sails

Last Voyages
by Nicholas Gray
Looking back at the lives and tragic loss of
some remarkable and well-known sailors

The First Indian
by Dilip Donde
The story of the first Indian solo
circumnavigation under sail

Golden Lily
by Lijia Xu
The fascinating autobiography from Asia's
first dinghy sailing gold medallist

more to follow

The Last SEA DOG

Jean-Luc Van Den Heede

with Didier Ravon

Translated by Riaan Smit

FERNHURST
BOOKS

Published in 2024 by Fernhurst Books Limited

The Windmill, Mill Lane, Harbury, Leamington Spa, Warwickshire, CV33 9HP,
UK Tel: +44 (0) 1926 337488 | www.fernhurstbooks.com

Translated from the French book:
Le dernier loup de mer par Jean-Luc Van Den Heede
© Éditions Stock, 2019

English translation © Riaan Smit, 2024

A catalogue record for this book is available from the British Library
ISBN 9781912621767

Front cover photograph: Christophe Favreau / GGR / PPL
Back cover photograph: Jean-Luc Van Den Heede

Designed & typeset by Daniel Stephen
Printed in India by Thomson Press India Ltd

Contents

To Don McIntyre who had the extraordinary idea of reviving a mythical race and managed it masterfully;
To Odile who accompanied me wholeheartedly in this adventure;
To Élisabeth and Éric who have so often seen their father leave;
And to my five grandchildren ...

Introduction

Departing from Les Sables-d'Olonne on 1st July 2018, the Golden Globe Race is a solo, non-stop circumnavigation created by Australian sailor and adventurer, Don McIntyre, to celebrate the 50th anniversary of the Golden Globe Challenge, won on 22nd April 1969, by the Englishman Robin Knox-Johnston. The 1969 race was the first single-handed, non-stop around the world sailing race ever.

At that time, nine participants competed, sponsored by the London-based *Sunday Times* newspaper. Six sailors abandoned the race due to damage to their boats, and Englishman Donald Crowhurst, ashamed of having lied about his positions since the day of his departure, committed suicide. One sailor, the legendary French single hander, Bernard Moitessier, rounded all four Capes, but when he turned north after Cape Horn – in second place behind Knox-Johnston – he decided to quit the race and continue sailing eastward to Tahiti in the Pacific Ocean, another half a world away. He was torn between facing frenzied accolades if he won the Race, and his quest for inner peace and contentment – the theme of his life as a sailor.

The slogan of GGR 2018 – and the 2022 Race held before the English translation of this book was published – was 'Sailing like it's 1968'. Eligible boats for the GGR were long-keel cruising monohulls designed 30 years ago or more. These sailboats, ranging from ten to eleven metres, were not allowed to carry technology not available in 1968 – no GPS, electronics, computers or autopilots.

Navigation was done using a sextant. Steering was either by hand or mechanical wind vanes. Like 1968, the rules permitted the use of an engine (but with fuel limited to 150 litres) and an electronic depth sounder. The only exception to these strict regulations was that competitors could use modern communication devices (satellite phones, distress beacons, etc.) for safety, but only in cases of extreme urgency, risking penalties or disqualification if used otherwise. Satellite technology helped track the entire fleet's position and progress online, creating a huge following for the GGR among fans.

17 boats participated in the second – 2018 – edition, but only five crossed the finish line. Dominating the race, Jean-Luc Van Den Heede returned to Les Sables-d'Olonne on 29th January 2019 after 212 days at sea (compared to 313 for Robin Knox-Johnston 50 years earlier).

Foreword

English edition – Don McIntyre

I first met Jean-Luc Van Den Heede (VDH) at the Sydney stop-over of the 1986 BOC Challenge, a solo race around the world over four legs. At the time I was Chairman and Founder of the Short-Handed Sailing Association of Australia, the Sydney host of the BOC, and was actively involved with all entrants. Jean-Luc's distinctive style and easy laugh matched my own. We quickly became good friends – me dreaming of doing the BOC and him dreaming of heading toward his first Cape Horn rounding. Over the past 37 years that friendship has grown in strength and character as we meet up in different parts of the world, watching and reminiscing about each other's adventures with admiration and plenty of laughs.

In January 2003, Jean Luc's *Adrien* was dismasted deep in the Southern Ocean during his attempt at an east-west circumnavigation record. I was not far away in Antarctica on my expedition ship *Sir Hubert Wilkins* and offered a tow north. He was in no immediate danger and, instead, sailed toward Tasmania under jury rig. We towed him in the last 40 miles into my home town, Hobart. He had hoped to return her to France on a ship loaded with 4,000 tons of onions, but his budget was tight. Instead, we lived together for seven weeks while a steel water pipe mast was built. He sailed home non-stop via Cape Horn.

For convenience, I was paying his bills to local suppliers while we built the new mast. Jean-Luc reimbursed me but many months later I realised he had overpaid me by $5,000. At the time, I was struggling with another expedition without sponsors. He replied: "Keep it; you owe me a bag of onions!"

When I announced the Golden Globe Race, I was not surprised that he called. "Wow, what have you done? Send me an entry form." It was a beautiful, emotionally-charged moment when he crossed the finish line at Les Sables D'Olonne as the winner of the GGR 2018 and collected the £5,000 prize. We both laughed as he declared: "You can forget the bag of onions now."

I now live in Les Sables D'Olonne in France, but I cannot master the French language and was disappointed not to be able to read his book when it was released in French. Now this superb translation has opened a whole new adventure to me, being able to absorb and understand the man behind the story, the man that has been my friend of so many years. I devoured every word with pure joy. This is a great read, an all-time classic that shows me a man not unlike Bernard Moitessier or Eric Tabarly.

He is very much his own person, an absolute inspiration, who has himself been inspired by others to live life with genuine passion. What a guy he is. A leader in life, a gentle giant who freely offers his time and experience to many and now shares it all in this classic English version. Thank you, my friend, for finally sharing and giving us non-French readers this opportunity. Bravo!

Foreword

French edition - Thomas Coville[1]

Having briefly been the fastest solo sailor around the globe, I am all for praising slow sailing, as highlighted by the Golden Globe Race during the winter of 2018/19. An around-the-world, non-stop race 'the old-fashioned way', based on old-school navigation methods – what a wonderful idea.

Here was the icing on the cake: one couldn't dream of a more fitting winner to promote its spirit. Jean-Luc Van Den Heede who has continually improved over the years, also gives the impression of being timeless. I don't know how old he is, how many years he has been sailing the seas or how many circumnavigations has he done. No one really knows and it doesn't matter.

Truth be told, Jean-Luc is 'outside' time. For him, neither the weather nor the passing of time truly matters. He belongs to my parents' generation, but his eyes sparkle like those of my children. His heart beats to the rhythm of

---

1. As the skipper of Sodebo, *Colville notably held the solo round-the-world record in 2016, completing it in 49 days and 3 hours, and has navigated around the Cape Horn eight times in races.*

the timeless ebbing and flowing of the sea. He 'lives' and he 'exists' in the simplest way, the most natural way in the world. Everything about him – his demeanour, his stature, his beard, his gaze – portrays honesty and integrity, two values that are timeless as well.

When VDH shakes your hand, the calluses that swell on his palms instantly reveal the authenticity of his approach and the audacity that is his to always want to go back 'there', to places where, precisely, lies do not exist. His voice, powerful and strong (when it's not singing ...), further adds to his sincerity. VDH stands out. VDH is striking.

But what strikes me the most about him are his choices. Perhaps therein lies the greatest of his merits. Because, truthfully, nothing predestined him. Neither his origins nor his family background. It is he, and he alone, who gave meaning to his life. His journey, both literally and figuratively, is simply incredible. It is all the more so because he imagined it alone, with a blend of pragmatism and passion that – by my standards – makes him a perfect 'free man'.

Chapter 1

Knock-down

GOLDEN°GLOBE°RACE

With the regularity of a cathedral bell, the waves crash against the starboard side of my boat. Powerful and vicious at the same time, they are not only violent, but the noise they create inside the dark cabin, turn it into a giant, echoing drum, further increase the level of threat and stress.

I'm on high alert. My boat rocks from side to side with the relentless determination of a metronome. This is not the first time I've faced a storm in these vast expanses of the Southern Pacific Ocean, far from any land. I have confidence in my boat, my floating safe. Nevertheless, the situation is worrisome, and it's only because I'm exhausted from the sleepless night before, that I manage to close one eye.

The respite is short-lived. Without warning, all at once, I'm thrown out of my bunk.

I roll and get squashed – like a fly – with all my weight (all 90 kilos of me) against a locker. Another second and I find myself stuck to the ceiling of the cabin. I'm half-conscious. Between dream and reality, I hear heaps of objects falling in an indescribable chaos and clamour, until the fridge door opens, releasing a cascade of provisions suddenly turned into projectiles.

As proof of the ferocity of this onslaught, the floor hatches, covering the batteries in the bilges, burst open despite the safety latch and the heavy bag of medical kit placed on top of them. There's no doubt, I've capsized, or at least performed a serious somersault. From 130-140 degrees? Or 150 degrees? It doesn't matter. My brave Rustler 36 was hit hard and took a blow, insidious but formidable. A real uppercut.

In an instant, the boat rolls in the opposite direction and I find myself upright again. By some miracle? The heavy keel, which represents almost half the weight of the boat on its own, played its role. Thank God. I move and regain my senses. Nothing seems to be broken, minor bruises perhaps, but no serious injuries.

In the chaos, I locate my boots and my wet weather jacket, climb on deck and peer into the darkness to see what damage has been done. The mast is still standing but the shrouds are slack and the mast rocks from side to side in the menacing Southern Pacific Ocean swells.

The canvas companionway dodger, which allows me to steer in shelter, is literally torn apart, its stainless-steel frame twisted like pieces of flimsy wire. I'm not feeling great, but I pull myself together. Now is not the time to be demoralised. I grab the flashlight at the bottom of the companionway steps and head back onto the deck for a thorough inspection.

The night is pitch black. The wind is blowing furiously. I

roughly estimate the waves to be around nine metres. I hang on to my bucking bronco of a boat. 'One hand for you, one hand for the boat'. The saying is more relevant than ever – especially since I'm not connected to any lifeline and I'm not wearing a lifejacket. I know it's not sensible, but I didn't have time to put it on, and anyway, in this situation, it wouldn't be very useful since I'm alone on board, and the nearest competitor is more than two weeks away from my position.

Flashback: 48 hours earlier, the race management[2] warned me about a strong storm. I even sensed some anxiety in the voice of Don McIntyre, the chief organiser of the Golden Globe Race, an old friend and seasoned sailor to whom I had lent my apartment overlooking the Bay of Sables-d'Olonne during my absence. Unlike me, he has access to all the weather forecasts, increasingly reliable and precise because of modern technology.

However, I just saw the needle of my barometer in free fall. Unfortunately, a sign (that does not lie) of bad weather to

---

2. *The Golden Globe Race officials responsible for enforcing the race regulations. The first Golden Globe Race – a single-handed, non-stop race around the world without outside assistance – was sailed in 1968. Only one sailor, Sir Robin Knox-Johnston, finished the race and became the first person to achieve this feat. Australian adventurer and solo sailor, Don McIntyre, revived the concept of the race for the 50th anniversary of the original in 2018. The third GGR was sailed in 2022, and won by a South African, Kirsten Neuschäfer.*

come. The radio amateurs I could speak to on my High Frequency radio, also confirmed a storm with southwest winds at Force 11 (103-117 km per hour or 64-72 miles per hour) gusting to Force 12 (over 117 km per hour, or 73 miles per hour – hurricane strength winds on the Beaufort Scale), accompanied by waves the size of a three-storey building.

I was sailing with a beam wind at about 2,000 miles (3,700 kilometres) from Cape Horn on this 5th November 2018, almost routine after 126 days of sailing since starting at Les Sables d'Olonne, France.

From time to time, a stronger and higher wave crashed into the hull and over the boat. Although *Matmut* is fairly stable under sail, thanks to its good beam width, I was worried but focused.

After completely lowering my mainsail, I was left with only a tiny scrap of canvas at the front. In anticipation of the worst, I made sure to secure and tie down everything that could be. However, I did need to rest as soon as possible. In a near sleep-walking state, I noted in my logbook, a 21 × 29.7cm school notebook with small squares and a red plastic cover: 'Wind 50 knots and more, sea is frothing!' Perhaps it was a coincidence or a premonition because for once, I left the small lamp above the chart table on and decided to lie down on the port bunk, the lee side.

My sleeping bag was damp, and my mattress as inviting as a garden bench in the rain.

The catastrophe has arrived. The long-feared capsizing and my rather eventful awakening. First assessment: The head of my Hydro vane self-steering gear, has suffered damage, but it still functions and steers my wounded vessel, which now zigzags between walls of raging water. Yes, the shrouds have loosened under the impact, and the mast has indeed been damaged at the port anchoring point of the shroud. To relieve it and potentially preserve it, I have no choice: I must position the boat in such a way to put the least side-ways strain on the mast.

This means I am steering north – the opposite direction to the route I had been following until now. I curse myself. I should have anticipated more, especially since I had a significant lead over the rest of the fleet and should not have stayed parallel to the waves for so long.[3]

What a fool! Now it's over; I will have to abandon the race. To make matters worse, the depression that has just pummelled me is not willing to let go. I have no way out. I know the rules forbid me from making a phone call – risking immediate disqualification[4] – but I can't help but grab my satellite phone to reassure my partner. She's in a meeting, but, thanks to the miracle of technology, she answers on her mobile.

I know I am breaking the Race rules, but I especially don't want Odile to learn about my distress and troubles from a third party, a member of the GGR organisation, or

---

3. *According to the GGR satellite tracker, Jean-Luc had about 8,960 miles to go to the finish in Les Sables-d'Olonne at the time of the knock down. The nearest competitor to him, at this point was Dutchman, Mark Slats, with 10,980 miles to go – a lead of over 2,000 miles.*
4. *Any external communication is considered 'outside assistance' which is against the Race rules and may result in disqualification. Given the circumstances, the organisation imposed an 18-hour penalty on VDH.*

worse still, from social media.

I briefly tell her that I am diverting to Puerto Montt in Chile and ask her to contact the local Beneteau dealer so that they can best organise my arrival and – and my withdrawal from the race.

I could continue my journey after repairs and compete in the Chichester Class, into which competitors drop if they have made one-stop or received outside assistance while at anchor. I don't even consider this option for a second. Perhaps, as a beginner during my first circumnavigation, I might have set off from Chile again, but now it's inconceivable. I would feel like I'm failing, wasting my time. This is my sixth and final solo circumnavigation race and arriving without stopping is my only goal.

Disheartened, I sit at the chart table, open my notebook, and in capital letters, with a blue pen, I write: 'CAPSIZE! SO THERE IT IS, THE JOURNEY IS OVER!' I no longer maintain my heading, no longer plot my course, and no longer mark any points on my soaked chart.

Time has stopped. What's the use! I no longer consider myself part of the race and feel like an outsider. I think about selling my boat there and then, getting a flight back home as soon as possible to spend Christmas with my family. Nevertheless, I start pondering on getting a new mast sent from France and continuing my adventure outside the race. I no longer know what to do! On the edge of the storm, my mind is boiling over! For sure, the mast is damaged but my margin of safety is still reasonably comfortable.

Soon, the wind shifts to the northwest, and the sea gradually calms down. The situation isn't ideal, but it allows me to consider some repairs. I prepare my tools and strap on a harness, the kind usually used by mountaineers. I'm no longer in my twenties. Climbing the mast is always perilous at sea, not to mention the descent.

Picture this: A still-choppy sea, swells of three metres or more, an 'old' man struggling to climb by sheer arm strength a telegraph pole more than ten metres high. I've experienced calmer situations.

I quickly confirm that the port shroud attachment has cut through the mast downwards like a can opener. The backing plate is torn off. My mast is in a sorry state. With nothing to lose, I'm going to try to stop further damage by lashing the shroud attachment to secure it from slipping down further.

I climb up again a second time, the following day, an operation that requires more than two hours of intense effort, with cramps and bruises as guaranteed bonuses because of the wildly swinging motion of the mast and the effort of holding on for dear life. I'm exhausted. I contemplate the most ingenious, or at least, the most effective solution. I need a very strong piece of rope of a few millimetres in diameter. The only piece suitable is the string of my trailing log – a device consisting of a small, spinning propeller on a long piece of rope, towed behind the boat. The number of times the propeller revolves is translated on an analogue dial as distance sailed.

For four days, I strengthen my mast and tighten all the shrouds, spending hours contorting myself, hanging onto a pole that seems to have taken on the role of a windscreen wiper.

This six centimetre gash at the shroud attachment on the mast is consuming me. But, after all, if I can secure the mast sufficiently, I might be able to pass Cape Horn and, at the same time, try to get a little closer to France. And if everything were to collapse despite my repairs, I could still set up a jury rig and reach shelter somewhere on the coast of South America. It's decided: I will continue!

I don't really know where I am because it's been six days since I've used my sextant.[5] But it doesn't bother me at all because where I am, in the middle of the vast Pacific, I have plenty of water to sail through. There's not an island or a rock in sight. I note in my logbook: 'Repair completed. Exhausted. No position, no log. Back underway at nearly 6 knots. Great!'

I finally take a sight but mess up the calculations like a novice in celestial navigation. I write, 'Not very good at maths (the maths teacher!). I'll take a noon sight tomorrow … if there's sunshine.' Nevertheless, I doodle a little smiley face – a smiling Jean-Luc. Another equally fierce depression is expected in 24 hours. Truly, the Pacific doesn't live up to its name. I can't wait to get around Cape Horn.

---

5. *Navigation instrument used to measure angles in relation to celestial bodies to determine a position on a chart by calculating latitude and longitude.*

Chapter 2

A solitary childhood

Coming out of the war, Amiens looked at best, like a field of ruins, at worst like a disaster zone. The bombings, German at the beginning of the conflict, and Allied in the lead-up to Liberation, had significantly destroyed the well-ordered layout of this peaceful provincial town. It was there, amidst a collection of shaky houses and plots strewn with rubble, that I was born on 8th June 1945 – exactly one month after the surrender of Nazi Germany.

Françoise, my older sister, arrived a year earlier, and Dominique, my second sister, three years later. Philippe, the youngest, would have an eight-year age gap from me. We were 'children of the war', as the saying goes, who would only later learn just how much the 'Little Venice of the North', according to Louis XV, suffered throughout the Second World War. Deprivation, occupation, repression – Amiens experienced it all during those dark years; not an ideal time to envision a future and dream of better days. Pierre Dufau and Auguste Perret were the famous architects appointed to bring some order to this endless chaos. There was a need for rebuilding, finding solutions and showing imagination.

My life started in slow motion. Despite being a robust baby weighing 4.2 kilograms at birth, from the very first hours, I didn't gain weight; on the contrary, I lost weight and regurgitated everything I swallowed. I was allergic to milk. Probably even to my mother Jacqueline's milk but I would never know. For some reason, that topic remained forever taboo. How many times did I hear my parents repeating: "There's no need to dredge up those stories; none of it matters!" I accepted it, without much desire to understand.

My mother was an only child, very Parisian, beautiful and refined, always well-groomed and well-dressed, with an impeccable education. Quite exceptional for the time, she held degrees in French, Latin and Greek. Born to teach, she couldn't escape that destiny. Early on, she fell in love with an 'entertainer' whom she married against her parents' wishes, who would have much preferred to see her marry a respectable man, a doctor or a lawyer. The situation led to long-standing tensions, especially between Jacqueline and her father.

The 'entertainer', my father, was named Roger. He was a good-looking, affable, amiable and a somewhat bohemian guy. He was a musician, received training as an electrician at the Boulle School[6] but for the most part, he earned a living by playing the piano in bars and clubs. He discovered jazz, recently brought over by the American liberators and was delighted with this find, which allowed him to indulge

---

6. *The Boulle School (École Boulle) is a college of fine arts and crafts and applied arts in Paris.*

in his love for parties and improvisation. During the war, like many of his peers, he should have been conscripted for the Compulsory Work Service (Service du Travail Obligatoire – STO) and sent to Germany with the blessing of the Vichy[7] regime. However, he managed – I don't know exactly how – to 'hide', constantly slipping through the cracks without being drafted or mobilised. As far as I know, he played an active role in the Resistance, which earned him a medal later, in Les Sables-d'Olonne.

My mother suspected her father of trying to denounce her husband, but even about this dark episode, I'm not certain. It's still one of the unresolved family secrets. A few weeks after my birth, my father was enlisted for a series of military operations near Lille.

During the time of his absence, my mother sent me away. Without initially informing him, because she could not contact him, my mother decided to send me to her parents who lived in the countryside, in Chaulnes, a small town of about a thousand inhabitants located in the Somme region, about 40 kilometres from Amiens. The reason? My health condition.

I was becoming increasingly thin, and it was urgent to get me back on my feet. The pastures around could only be beneficial for my recovery. The family doctor's opinion which was quite alarming, probably weighed heavily on the decision to move me away from my biological parents in favour of my grandparents. It probably also relieved

---

7. *The Vichy regime was the collaborationist ruling regime or government in Nazi-occupied France during the Second World War.*

my mother of feeling like she was 'abandoning' me in a way. That isn't too strong a word. When Jeanne, my grandmother, picked me up at her place, I weighed only 2.7 kilograms. I was so light that, when she lifted my crib, she doubted whether I was inside.

Initially, my grandparents couldn't get me to swallow anything other than sweetened water. My milk allergy was very real. Proof of that: 74 years later, I still don't drink milk. Substitutes had to be found, and patience had to be mustered. After five weeks, I reached a milestone (my first!) by regaining some semblance of an appetite.

They say I'm a survivor. Furthermore, today psychiatrists might also think that I could have served as a 'sacrifice', so that my mother could be somehow forgiven by her father for marrying a man who didn't meet her family's criteria.

My two sisters, too, had tumultuous journeys. The elder, Françoise, was asked to leave home early on to make a living, and Dominique 'freed' herself while still a minor. Settled near Barcelona, managing a nightclub with her then-fiancé, she resumed her studies at the age of 23 and bravely pursued a medical degree shortly afterwards. Dominique became a psychiatrist. She always had many questions and her perspective deserves to be heard. Mine is more down-to-earth. How can I sort through my memories? Why interpret them? I'm only reporting what has been confided to me. And to be honest, even with hindsight, even as part of the memory exercise I'm subjecting myself to today, I don't think I want to know. I couldn't care less.

What I'm certain of, though, is that I was, for my grandfather, the son he had always dreamed of having.

Arsène was a cultured and hardworking man, passionate about politics, a radical-socialist, following the principles of Marshall Pétain[8], whose motto 'Work, family, homeland' he appreciated above all – a motto that has gone down in history for better or for worse.

For him, Germany was not an enemy but a model. After his death, I found and recovered boxes of archives. Carefully labelled and dated files, 6 x 9 photos, and letters where he didn't hesitate to refer to his son-in-law – my father – as a 'poor type'. Clearly, he harboured complete contempt for him throughout his life, but fortunately, he never spoke to me about it.

I never felt any rejection or ostracism from my grandfather; on the contrary, he lavished me with attention, if not love. His wife was sterner, more abrasive, but it must be said that her life was far from enviable. As I mentioned, it was not a prosperous time and we lacked everything. Except for shopping, my grandmother rarely left her home and spent her time with often thankless household chores.

My grandfather was unfaithful to her incessantly. Looking back, I must have known a few of his mistresses. My grandmother's later years were not joyful. Afflicted with Parkinson's disease, she remained confined to her home, cared for until the end by her husband. Barely after mourning her, Arsène remarried a much younger woman, so young that she gave birth to a daughter in 1970, after my own daughter Élisabeth was born.

---

8. *Marshall Philippe Pétain led the French pro-Nazi Vichy government in World War II.*

Funny family. Françoise, my elder sister who became a nurse, was also 'placed' but this time with Louise, our paternal grandmother, before being 'returned' about a year later. Her husband, our grandfather Jules, of Flemish origin – hence my surname – was the last of 11 children. He was much older than Louise and passed away when my father was seven years old due to a fall from a ladder. (I never knew him, of course.) Louise found herself alone managing a business.

My parents had their share of struggles too. Despite her qualifications, my mother couldn't find a suitable job, and my father had a hard time securing gigs.

On our family record, he wrote 'farmers' as their profession. Indeed, Jacqueline and Roger once owned a mushroom farm near Amiens. They survived, if not prospered, but they never openly discussed their difficulties, let alone the choice they made to 'place' their first two children.

Nevertheless, I wasn't unhappy with my grandparents. Far from it. I was much loved and somewhat the centre of their world. I grew up and regained my strength. They 'rescued' me and cared for me as if I were delicate porcelain. I wasn't allowed to exert myself and was exempt from physical activities at school. Even though they remained at odds with my parents, I remember fondly that they allowed me to visit my parents for the first time when I must have been six or seven years old. It was in Paris, for a weekend and I must have stayed over with them.

Two years earlier, Arsène had been appointed as a receiver, a tax collector in the third division of the Treasury.

He had made an impression. Always well-dressed, perfectly groomed moustache, he was a charmer. His subordinates followed his lead but also appreciated his charisma. With his new position, he had left Chaulnes to settle in Amiens, right at the top of Rue Charles-Dubois.

I was five years old. The brick house was austere but comfortable, and my grandfather spent weekends tinkering with it to make it more pleasant. I was mostly alone. My grandparents didn't receive visitors and lived in isolation. They had a spacious living-dining room, but they never used it. The furniture was always covered with old, yellowed and worn-out sheets. There was also an upright piano, dusty and untouched by anyone.

We occupied the kitchen and the back kitchen. There was a table against the wall, three chairs, a shelf for my school things, an aquarium where my goldfish frolicked, and that was about it. Since I often did my homework in my grandfather's home office, I escaped by drawing trains and boats.

I didn't particularly excel at school, but my grandparents didn't pressure me. They provided a quiet and comforting environment, which I cherished. Mr Petit, my teacher, was clear: "If he manages to pass the elementary certificate that would be an achievement!"

To access the bedroom I shared with my grandparents – a partition had been removed so they could constantly monitor my health – I had to walk through the unoccupied living room that smelt musty. This odour, a mix of an old church and a damp cellar, would haunt me for years.

Winters were harsh in the Somme region, and the coal-fired central heating was always running. When I wasn't playing with my toy train – my second passion after drawing – I spent hours daydreaming in what seemed like a large garden, on a raft made of wooden planks, a broomstick and a piece of cloth. I virtually sailed away.

Today, I have no doubt: My love for boats was born in that green corner and on that makeshift raft that, fortunately, never touched the water.

I could point to another twist of fate: Jules Verne[9] himself lived at the bottom of this street, just a few hundred metres from my grandparents' house. He even died there in March 1905, 40 years before I was born. But even though this proximity is remarkable, I wasn't aware of it when I was an adolescent.

More than the gilded-edged epics of the brilliant writer, what obsessed me at the time was the desire to break free from the loneliness I suffered. No visitors, no friends. I didn't really complain; I accepted my circumstances, like an obligation, like a fate.

Outside school and vacations, my outings were rare. Upon my insistence, I was allowed to attend the home matches of Amiens Sporting Football Club every two weeks. The club played not far from there at the Moulonguet stadium. In reality, the matches didn't matter much to me. What counted for me was playing on the adjacent field, in secret, in the company of a few classmates.

---

9. *French author, particularly famous for adventure novels such as* Around the World in Eighty Days *and* Journey to the Centre of the Earth.

Since I had to avoid sweating – a sign that would give me away to my grandparents – I opted to be the goalkeeper. Without wearing those thick cotton and compressed felt knee pads and not hesitating to dive on a sometimes-frozen field in winter, it was also important to conceal any potential injuries. My grandparents had to see nothing was amiss. And that was the case.

The discovery of the sea happened in parallel. Born in Berck-Ville in the Pas de Calais, my grandfather Arsène would rent a very small apartment in Berck-Plage, the nearby seaside resort, every summer. According to him, it was the best place in the world to breathe in the sea air.

Indeed, the town hosted numerous sanatoria. On the beach, there were tidal pools, those water reservoirs at low tide that invited children to splash around and build ports and sandcastles. The first toy I have a wonderful memory of is a small white plastic sailboat with significant ballast that helped it maintain its course. I named it *Nayouk*. I didn't have to search far for a name; it was written on the box. I adored it and spent hours watching it glide on the breeze.

However, it would end its nautical career in a very sad way. When the vacation was over, and we returned to our house in Amiens, my grandmother Jeanne went to fetch her slippers. As she was about to put them on, she discovered a mouse in one of them, screamed, grabbed me suddenly by the hip, and jumped onto a chair and then onto the table. Consequently, I dropped my boat, and its keel shattered on the tiled floor. Heroically, my grandfather dispatched the rodent with a sweep of his broom but couldn't do anything for my boat. Despite my attempts at patching, it leaked from all sides, and it would never sail again. To replace it, I chose a sturdy red wooden fishing boat that I would continually modify with a keel and three hinged masts, but it never quite matched *Nayouk*'s performance.

At Berck-Plage, amphibious vehicles from the war would regularly land on the beach to take vacationers on brief sea excursions. I was fascinated by this spectacle and would stand for hours watching them depart and return.

My parents, sisters and brother rarely joined us during vacations. My mother didn't particularly enjoy the windy climate of Pas-de-Calais, and my father was busy covering the Tour de France as a sound technician for French Radio. It didn't matter; I made the most of every opportunity. I crafted a makeshift land yacht from a stroller, using bits of wood and a piece of patched-up fabric. Since it was too heavy for me, I designated my younger brother Philippe as the test pilot, which he only half appreciated. My mother, who was following my experiments, wasn't thrilled either.

A few years later, my grandfather bought me an aeroplane ticket – I believe it was on a propeller-driven Viscount – to Bordeaux. It was my first time meeting my biological family while they were on vacation near Arcachon. I was barely ten years old and brimming with curiosity about the world.

Chapter 3

The call of the Golden Globe Race

GOLDEN°GL⊙BE°RACE

At home, it's a ritual I perform every morning when I wake up – much like when I finish my night in a half-awake state before heading back up on deck to take my first watch. Sitting on a stool in a corner of my living space, which I've arranged to resemble a boat's chart table, I instinctively open my laptop. This routine never leaves me. At sea, I note my position, course, speed, wind direction and strength, wave height and the type of sails used. On land, I check my schedule for the day, go through my emails, and respond to the most urgent ones.

Visitors who come to my place for the first time immediately notice the absence of boundaries between my home and my boat. Same objects, same atmosphere, same concerns.

Here, I don't display any medals or trophies. Instead, a multitude of nautical charts under glass are hanging on the wall. Perhaps out of nostalgia or obsession but probably a bit of both. Unless it's related to the world maps and other French maps that accompanied me in the classroom during my time as a teacher.

All in all, these charts from the SHOM [10] or the Admiralty, scribbled and worn like old parchments, are my trophies. On one of them – the waters around Cape Horn – I've amused myself by tracing all my passages over the past 40 years with four different coloured pens, day by day, hour by hour. More than a collector's whim, these accumulated trajectories serve as a perfect reminder, a means to recall all the storms, all the choices, all the approaches, before the very real relief of a trap that hasn't been nicknamed the 'Cape of Hardship' entirely by chance. A few polaroids from my only landing on Horn Island with the lighthouse keeper's family are tucked into the lower part of the frame. An additional piece of evidence that undoubtedly adds to my connection with the place.

My home is my treasure trove of maritime memories and experiences. Each of my visitors can experience it. On another map of Antarctica and the Southern Ocean, as seen from the South Pole, I've marked all the routes of my various circumnavigations. It's quite a traffic jam.

Further along, I've lined up three models of my iconic racing boats – *36-15 Met*, *Sofap Helvim-Algimouss* and *Adrien* – alongside various prints of iceberg photos taken during my very first Vendée Globe, now more than 30 years ago. The edges are curling a bit and the photos have faded with time. Every time I come face to face with these breath-taking images, I think of the risks I took back then. Pure

---

10. *Hydrographique et Océanographique de la Marine, the compiler of these nautical charts.*

madness!

As for the books that fill the library, they are primarily accounts of circumnavigators or their biographies. Some were given to me, like the one by the American Joshua Slocum[11], written by his own son.

I've had 20 boats. They're almost all there, in an informal jumble, in half-models, miniatures, photos, wood, neatly lined up. A bit forgotten, a bit worn, a bit battered but they tell the tales of incredible adventures, absolutely fitting in this perfect maritime setting, where seagulls, carried by the offshore wind, glide just a stone's throw from the balcony, sometimes threatening, under the gusts, to crash against my glass windows.

On this April morning in 2015, I stuck to my routine: A cup of tea, going through my emails, deleting spam and discarding unwanted ones. One message immediately caught my attention, that of Jean-Marie, a loyal friend I met, as fortuitously as comically, a dozen years ago.

At that time, 2003, I had just abandoned my attempt to set a record circumnavigating the world against the prevailing winds, from east to west. The mast of my large monohull, *Adrien*, had broken while I was sailing south of Australia. I had found a replacement for it, made from odds and ends from pieces of fire hoses salvaged in Tasmania. It was a makeshift solution, bound to rust, but I had no choice – it was the only way I had found to bring my 25.70-metre monohull back to France.

---

11. *The first sailor to complete a solo circumnavigation – from 1895 to 1898 – with numerous stopovers.*

It was then that I received a message from a guy I knew nothing about, living in Angers. His name was Jean-Marie Patier; he was the director of a private school, an economics teacher and an occasional sailor like many others. Despite having no experience with the open sea or the Southern Ocean, he was the first to come up with an offer of help. But what exactly was he proposing?

He wanted to join me in Hobart, where I had landed, and accompany me as crew for the return journey. The idea intrigued me and appealed to me so Jean-Marie hopped on the first flight to Australia.

My loved ones warned me. In their eyes, taking on a complete stranger, someone no one in the sailing community had ever heard of was just plain crazy. According to them, I'd have to deal with an entirely inexperienced 'burden' on top of my technical challenges. Some even predicted the worst: A brawl in the middle of the ocean, me going overboard, and him taking possession of the boat. However, I didn't back down. We'd see.

From our very first meeting, we hit it off. Perhaps our shared backgrounds as educators naturally brought us closer? Even though the weather was against us, even though Jean-Marie was encountering the rough weather of the 50th latitudes for the first time, even though he got scared, he handled every situation admirably. He had faith in me and was a good companion. After 77 days at sea, we became the best of friends.

One year later, in Les Sables-d'Olonne, I introduced Jean-Marie to Catherine Chabaud, to whom I had chartered my 'red cigar'[12] a few years earlier. She became the first woman to complete a solo, round-the-world race during the 1996/97 Vendée Globe. A few months later, the two lovebirds joined forces, united for good and welcomed a son named Côme, to whom I am godfather. Opening a matchmaking agency crossed my mind for a split second.

On a more serious note, on that fateful day in April 2015, Jean-Marie shared some information he had found on an English website: My Australian friend Don McIntyre's ambition to launch a recreation of the Golden Globe Challenge, a solo circumnavigation race sponsored by the *Sunday Times* in 1968/69.

It was the first solo, non-stop around-the-world race – a challenge never before imagined. Nine entrants started, but only one finished, (Sir Robin Knox-Johnston), one sailor famously abandoned the race (Bernard Moitessier), another committed suicide during the race (Donald Crowhurst) and a third sailor committed suicide afterwards (Nigel Tetley).

The myth, the legend, one of the greatest feats in the history of competitive sailing, Jean-Marie's email is brief and to the point but ends with a bombshell: 'This race is for you!' I was stunned.

At the time in the late 1960s, of course, I had followed that incredible circumnavigation and have since read all the books on the subject. I didn't miss any films or documentaries, especially the poignant BBC documentary

---

12. *The boat was built in 1991 for the Vendée Globe of 1992/93. It was much narrower than the trend for very wide maximum beam Open 60 class boats at the time, hence the nickname of 'red cigar'.*

about Crowhurst filming himself and confessing to having lied about his positions.

What if Jean-Marie was right? I'm not one to get carried away easily, but I acknowledged this opportunity, especially since the organisers were specifying that candidates for this adventure would have to sail under the same conditions as the 1968/69 race – without GPS, electronics, computers or autopilots.

I didn't have very defined short- or medium-term plans, and I was fortunate not to be constrained by any commitments. There was no doubt that this idea deserved a detailed study. A sixth solo circumnavigation in a 'vintage' style boat excited me, but I was not there yet, far from it.

One, I was 70 years old. Two, I didn't have a boat. And three, considering the type of sailboats for the race – slow – it was going to last for nearly eight months. I needed some time to think.

My outward optimism can be deceptive. I'm very pragmatic and full of doubts. Throughout my life, I've needed to weigh the pros and cons, digest and put my emotions on the back burner.

In the days that followed, many images and memories came to mind: 1968[13], I was 23 years old, a student. This circumnavigation went somewhat unnoticed in France, but within the sailing community, everyone – including myself

---

13. *May 1968 in France was the start of a period of civil unrest lasting seven weeks with demonstrations, general strikes, and the occupation of universities and factories. It caused the economy of France to come to a halt.*

– was amazed by the pioneering spirit of the venture. No sailor had ever dared such a feat – to sail solo, non-stop around the world without outside assistance around the Cape of Good Hope, Cape Leeuwen, and the ultimate, Cape Horn, and back up the Atlantic to Europe. No doubt, these nine adventurers were heading off into the complete unknown.

They had the option to set sail from and return to any port north of the 45th parallel, with a window of only five months between June and October 1968. I inevitably identified with Frenchman Loïck Fougeron, with whom I would become friends in Lorient many years later. I also saw a reflection of myself in Bernard Moitessier, the other Frenchman in the race at the helm of his impressive *Joshua*.

Apart from nautical magazines like *Bateaux* and *Les Cahiers du Yachting*, the French press didn't pay much attention to this round-the-world race. I spent hours dissecting every article, every piece of information, and even more so, the drawings of the nine competing sailboats. I scrutinised the CVs of all the competitors, discovering that many of them had hardly ever sailed before.

The British press playfully mocked Robin Knox-Johnston, believing that this young naval officer had no chance on his old, run-down boat. I had already read everything by Moitessier. I followed his progress through the messages he sent, either from small boats he cast adrift along the way or with a catapult when he encountered a cargo ship. One of these 'messages in a bottle' even made the cover of *Paris Match*. A friend had given me that collector's issue, and I keep it safely stored in a drawer with the rest of my cherished sailing memories, having a prominent place in my extensive library.

I adore his philosophy, that authenticity and the strong sense of a free man that characterises him. One of his sentences – 'I am a citizen of the most beautiful country[14] in the world' – has left a lasting mark on me. After rounding Cape Horn, he seemed destined for an expected triumph if he sailed his sturdy red ketch back to England after rounding Cape Horn. But he chose to shun success and adulation and continued his journey around the Cape of Good Hope again, heading deep into the Pacific, all the way to Tahiti because, as he wrote, he wanted to 'save his soul' and break free once and for all from the money-mad society he had left behind.

In the wake of the events of May 1968 in France, his decision took on a symbolic significance. His remarkable book, *La Longue Route*[15], published a year later, had a profound impact on me.

I also have boundless affection and deep respect for Robin Knox-Johnston. Not only was he the only one of the nine entrants at the start to complete the circumnavigation (in 313 days at the helm of a tiny wooden boat he had built in India), but he was leading the race when Moitessier decided to drop out. Who knows if, despite a significant speed differential, he wouldn't have held onto the lead until the end[16], knowing that the sailors were also racing against

---

14. *The sea.*
15. *Available in English as* The Long Way.
16. *A letter from Moistessier to Robin Knox-Johnston indicates that he did not think he would have overtaken Robin.*

the clock?

It's an understatement to say that this race excited me. It didn't determine my vocation, but its twist-filled storyline certainly influenced me. For me, the sea had become a promise capable of fulfilling my wildest dreams and extreme aspirations.

Chapter 4

Birth of a dual calling

As my grandmother's health deteriorated, and after an unpromising first term in the fifth grade, my parents decided to take me back with them. I knew that my lifelong protectors were sad, but I promised to visit them even if it meant cycling: the 130 kilometres separating Amiens from Neuilly-sur-Seine didn't scare me and I had no complaints about my new home. We lived in a spacious apartment on Rue Devès, close to the botanical gardens. I enrolled in Lycée Pasteur, a high school which wasn't too far away either. When it came to mathematics and science, there was no problem: I did very well, and even more enthusiastically, as I had a crush on my maths teacher in the 6th grade. However, I didn't shine in other subjects.

My parents were rather cool, as young people say today. No jarring constraints, but also no excessive displays of affection. Two years went by at the pace of a lazy, peaceful river. With more freedom than in Amiens, I went out as I pleased, sometimes hanging around with less-than-reputable boys. My grades suffered, especially since I only tried in the subjects I enjoyed. Not only were we unruly, but we were also thoughtless. My parents often despaired.

Our French teacher was called Mr Abramovitch. We nicknamed him 'Abraham'. It wasn't very clever, but that was our age. One day, we came up with nothing smarter than to disassemble the desks and benches in the classroom. Naturally, everything rocked and wobbled, and the entire class started swaying while singing "Maman, les petits bateaux" (Mummy, the little boats). Everyone was in on it, but 'Abraham' only identified one culprit, and, of course, his wrath was directed at me. The joke had gone on long enough. It ended up in the principal's office with punishment, made even more bitter by the fact that my mother, herself a teacher, worked at the same school.

My good maths grades no longer sufficed, and I was expelled shortly after. I found the situation hard to bear. I may not have been entirely innocent in this story, but my status as a 'teacher's son' clearly didn't help me. I learnt my lesson: when I became a teacher myself, I always kept my children away from the schools where I worked.

My father handled the situation as best as he could and began searching for a new school. Given my report cards, this proved to be difficult. Without a prestigious school to go to, I ended up in a private school in Froyennes, Belgium, just a stone's throw from the border with France and about 15 kilometres from Roubaix.

This school had an undisputed reputation. The atmosphere was regulated and discipline was strict. It seemed that a few 'tightening of screws' wouldn't hurt me. Upon discovering the austere buildings surrounded by four high walls, with a chapel in the middle, I felt like I was entering a prison.

Right away, and knowing my inclination for Maths, the headmaster made me take a short exam. It was futile. I made mistakes as if on purpose. At the end of the day, his assessment was clear: "Young man, you clearly don't want to be here."

He understood. Fortunately for me, he knew of a private boarding school in Livarot in the Pays d'Auge that might suit me, and he advised my father to consider this alternative. The school, Saint-Joseph, prepared students for the CAP (Certificat d'aptitude professionnelle) and the BEPC (Brevet d'Etudes du Premier Cycle) – qualifications during the final two or three years of school in France.

I was not overjoyed, far from it, but the atmosphere didn't bother me either. The headmaster, Mr Grasset, who also taught French, was a colourful character, dressing haphazardly, unkempt, no style, and prone to spitting while speaking – very far from the usual standards of a school principal, but quite likable.

At an age when one is searching for role models and directions to follow, his non-conformism didn't displease me. I had no idea what I wanted to do with my life. At one point, I even imagined becoming a priest or a missionary. Just for a while, though.

Before Livarot, if I attended Mass regularly, it was more out of obligation than conviction. At the time, it was necessary to have a form signed after each service, listing one's 'commitments to God'. I went through the motions but didn't attend the entire Mass. I was there at the beginning to be seen, and again at the end to prove my presence. I wasn't a believer, but a practitioner due to circumstances.

In this caring boarding school, I regained my interest in studies and became a good student again. I was even entrusted with my first responsibilities. It was a complete turnaround, an unexpected opportunity. The end of the year approached. The supervisor for the 5th and 6th grades was not up to the task and often absent. To make matters worse, he was beaten up by kids, dressed as ghosts during a carnival. He took it hard and decided to throw in the towel. The position was vacant and I decided that if there was no other solution, I would take it.

In the eyes of the younger kids, who were only two or three years younger than me, I was 'VDH' or 'Vu D'en Haut' ('Seen from Above') due to my significantly taller stature. My 'scrawny' years were a distant memory. I was 15 years old, standing at 1.87 metres, and paradoxically, I was a student just like them.

I made an impression and felt very comfortable with my new responsibilities. A significant advantage was that my new status offered me a number of privileges, including a room, admittedly as comfortable as a monk's cell, but more private than the common dormitory.

Above all, I felt good in the company of my 'subjects'. I probably benefitted from a natural authority – was I not the starting goalkeeper for the local senior football team? But, more importantly, a relationship of trust naturally developed between us. I was almost becoming popular as a prefect. The only downside was that I had to change schools again, as Saint-Joseph only offered classes up to the end of the third year.

During my free time, I read a lot, especially adventure and sea stories. It was during this time that I discovered the works of Alain Gerbault[17], Joshua Slocum, Vito Dumas[18], Jacques-Yves Le Toumelin[19] and Marcel Bardiaux[20] – but also those of Alain Bombard[21], who used to buy cheese from the creamery where my paternal grandmother worked.

I read and reread *Les Navigateurs Solitaires* by Jean Merrien[22] (alias René de La Poix de Fréminville, a staunch Breton nationalist) so many times that I could recite it by heart. I'll never forget that Christmas gift.

I start sailing on small, light boats – Simoun, Vaurien and Flibustier – the introductory dinghies of that time. My home port was Villers-sur-Mer, between Houlgate and Deauville, where we now spent our vacations and rented a small seasonal lodging. This destination wasn't chosen randomly. My father, a sound engineer, now worked for Europe 1 Radio. Every summer, he was assigned to the Deauville Racecourse with Ben, the famous in-house columnist and indispensable expert in horse race forecasting.

Regularly, my mother made me work on my English. It was an exercise that took its toll on me but mattered to me

---

17. *Alain Gerbault – French sailor and writer.*
18. *Vito Dumas – Argentine solo sailor and adventurer.*
19. *Jacques-Yves Le Toumelin – French circumnavigator and author.*
20. *Marcel Bardiaux – French sailor and first to cross Cape Horn east to west.*
21. *Alain Bombard – French scientist and politician (Euro MP) who sailed across the Atlantic with no provisions.*
22. *Available in English as* Lonely Voyagers.

as well. I was only allowed to go out once I had completed my page of vocabulary and grammar exercises, all topped off with a daily quiz. Considering the promises that came with this 'carrot', my progress was undoubtedly impressive.

The rest of the routine was unchanged: once the cramming session was over, I would hop on my bike and ride to Deauville, seven or eight kilometres away, where I'd spend the entire afternoon on the quay. There, I would watch the ballet of boats entering and leaving the harbour, help the sailors dock, unload and set sail again. I daydreamed, escaped and felt the urge to join in with these kinds of activities and, even more out of reach, yearned to head out to sea.

I loved nothing more than gazing at the clouds coming from the west and the gusts swirling above the harbour. I would close my eyes and listen to the halyards tapping against the masts. Occasionally, my patience was rewarded and I would be offered a chance to go aboard as a 'deckhand'.

For four years, every summer, a ritual took shape where I balanced summer homework with odd jobs. I always had a need to be resourceful and independent. I even worked for a local photographer, doing some wedding or baptism chores, or, even more motivating, covering the Miss Villers-sur-Mer beauty pageant. Each day, with my moped, I would go on a tour of the campsites to collect rolls of film and distribute photo prints. As time went on, I started to envision a career related to the world of the sea. With my friend Pierre Bonnefoy, we passed the time talking about boats for hours, sharing stories of distant voyages.

The idea had taken root. I mentioned it to my parents, who suggested I take some tests. The examiner welcomed me and expressed concern about my aspirations for a career in merchant navy. She hesitated, mentioning that it's a competitive field. Failing to see myself on the bridge of a cargo ship with a cap and gold epaulettes, I simply decided to become a teacher. My mother did everything to dissuade me.

In the meantime, I needed to get back to my studies. I found myself in the second year at the Frémont Institution in Lisieux, Calvados. I hadn't abandoned my educator role and took turns leading outings, supervising study sessions and enjoying assuming other responsibilities. I was well-regarded and found genuine satisfaction in becoming increasingly involved. I wondered if this was the beginning of a vocation. I wanted to pursue a useful profession, and teaching seemed to align with that intention. Why not become a gym teacher? After all, I was quite involved in sports.

I barely had time to voice this wish when I fell seriously ill, suffering from dietary and digestive problems. Following this setback, I failed my first year Baccalaureate exam and was forced to repeat a year. To regain my health, I left the boarding school, returned to my family home in Neuilly-sur-Seine, and was admitted to the first year Baccalaureate course at the Frémont Institution in Lisieux. It was a period of doubt and uncertainty about my future career, but my interest in teaching continued to grow. I was on a quest for a profession that felt meaningful and useful for the future.

I enrolled at the Lycée Saint-Sulpice on Rue d'Assas

in the sixth arrondissement of Paris. With a Maths score of 19.5 out of 20 in the first round of the Baccalaureate exams, I got a sweet taste of revenge. My parents recognised this achievement and decided to reward me with a sailing course at Les Glénans, the leading sailing school in France.

In the Cornouaille region on the west coast of Brittany, I discovered the wild paradise of the island of Drénec, where the most famous sailing school in France, founded by Philippe Viannay in the immediate post-war period, is located.

From the start, I appreciated the sense of community there, the simplicity of the place and my initial experiences on a Caravelle sailing boat. I felt in perfect harmony with the surroundings, the activities and the instructors, no matter who they were. The connection was so strong that I pestered my parents to let me go on a second course, this time on, a Mousquetaire, a small 6.48-metre plywood cruising sailboat. Coastal navigation between the islands of Groix and Tudy, wild anchorages at Port-Manech or Bélon were pure joy. Diligent and more motivated than ever, I even earned a scholarship for a third course, this time to become an instructor – at Penfret during the following Easter holidays.

Before returning to class, I made a big decision: if I didn't pass my second Baccalaureate, I wouldn't repeat it but would enter the Maistrance School in Toulon which trains non-commissioned officers for the French Navy. It seemed to me to be the best way to get to travel around the world and fulfil a dream buried within me since forever.

Despite my parents' reluctance, I boasted about it,

knowing that I would definitely be accepted because at that time, they took candidates with the first Baccalaureate and a high school pass. The escape plan was obvious – except that I passed my Baccalaureate on the retake and thus, I didn't go to Maistrance.

Ironically, many years later, my son Éric, instead of taking his BTS exam, told me his wished to join ... Maistrance! I laughed and told him my story, which is identical to his in every way, except that he really gets in and ends up sailing on the schooner *L'Étoile* and circumnavigating on the *Jeanne-d'Arc* before becoming a watch officer on the aircraft carrier *Charles-de-Gaulle*.

As for me, I was determined to become a teacher. My parents only accepted this if I joined a programme that required me to work for the State for a certain number of years as compensation. Scared of owing something to someone, especially the State, I refused.

Here I was in a tiny apartment above my parents' place in Neuilly, juggling multiple odd jobs to make ends meet. I enrolled in the science faculty at Jussieu University, attending evening classes, but struggling to organise my schedule. As a day supervisor at the Saint-Louis School on Rue de Monceau, a night worker at the postal sorting office in Neuilly and an estate agent on top of that, I had a lot on my plate. I also sold magazines door-to-door for an hour here and there.

Through the power of conviction and persuasion, my bank granted me a loan that, with my grandfather's guarantee, allowed me to buy a small apartment on Rue de Torcy, in the 18th arrondissement of Paris, near the diverse and lively neighbourhood of La Chapelle. This was in 1966. Then, I mainly sailed as a crew member every weekend, but I dreamt of having my own boat.

Chapter 5

Searching for the five-legged sheep

GOLDEN°GL⋂BE°RACE

I would turn 70 in a month, and I'm happy with my life, which is jam-packed. I raced on weekends with friends on my Feeling 1040 *Algimouss*, discovering new horizons on cruises with my partner Odile. I enjoyed playing in my rock band 'Globalement Vôtre' ('Overall Yours'), giving lectures all over France and Europe. Nevertheless, this project of an around-the-world voyage in old-school boats haunted me. It was even giving me insomnia. Just for the sake of it, I thought about it for another week ... but I'd already decided, I wanted to participate in the Golden Globe Race.

I'd already studied 20 boats that could meet the specifications set out in the Notice of Race (NOR – the rules of the Race). The approved sailboats must be less than 10.90 metres, be from a production series – in other words, not specially built for the GGR – and, above all, have a long keel with an attached rudder in line with it.

I used to own *Altair*, a superb 10.70-metre wooden boat that met these criteria, but it was so long ago that I can't remember how to set it up to get the most out of it. I remember sitting on the balcony of my apartment on the top floor of a building with an unobstructed view of the Sables-d'Olonne channel, the Barges lighthouse and the Nouch Sud cardinal buoy that marks the arrival of the Vendée Globe, and temporarily forgetting the panorama whilst I surfed for hours on the Internet searching for the right boat.

I immediately ruled out boats designed between 1950 and 1960, as they were too old, and those built outside Europe, fearing tedious import administrative procedures. I knew it didn't exist, but I was on the hunt for the famous 'five-legged sheep'. A boat that was not too heavy but had a substantial ballast ratio. A boat that was not too wide but not too narrow either, even though I'd always favoured narrower boats – *Let's Go, Éclipse, 36-15 Met, Sofap Helvim*. The right compromise seemed to be the Rustler 36.

Here I was in Falmouth, England, knocking on the door of the shipyard where Kim Holman and Don Pye designed the Rustler in 1980. I unrolled my CV, explaining that I wanted to do a new solo circumnavigation race – my sixth – and only wished to acquire a hull, deck and its interior fittings, knowing that I would buy the rest (mast, rigging, sails) from the suppliers I had been dealing with for 30 years between La Rochelle and Lorient. The complete boat was out of reach (close to €400,000), but even a bare hull was equally unaffordable.

A dead end! I was both annoyed and frustrated. So, I moved on, with the idea of settling for a used Rustler. I combed the south coast of England – Falmouth, Plymouth and Portsmouth – and finally found the 'rare bird' from a very nice, retired couple. Their cruiser, dating from 1990, was named *Mojito* – the name inherited by them from its first Spanish owner. I realise instantly that it has been well taken care of. The coverings on the cushions, the impeccable varnish, the two carved wooden columns at the bottom of the companionway resembling two very ugly table legs, the clean and dry lockers containing a multitude of bags, and even bags within bags, all testified to a lot of care and attention. I struck a deal for €75,000 and brought the boat to Les Sables in August. Lifting out of the water and an overall check were necessary and as there were no bad surprises, I could start training.

I was getting familiar with my new vessel, filling up school notebooks, jotting down everything that needed to be modified, while respecting the NOR – a document as detailed as it was indigestible at 65 pages. The rules for the first Vendée Globe Challenge in 1989/90 were on a single A4 page!

We were being invited to sail in the old-fashioned way, but the safety regulations were stringent – in the Anglo-Saxon style. In addition to an ocean-approved liferaft, the arsenal of safety equipment required on board is impressive: an electronic depth sounder, four distress beacons, three VHF[23] radios, a single-sideband radio (SSB)[24] for communication among competitors and with ham radio operators, two

---

23. *Very High Frequency. Fixed or portable radio for short-distance communication with land and rescue centres on channel 16.*
24. *Single Sideband Radio allowing long-distance land-sea and sea-sea communication.*

Iridium satellite phones, but only for contacting the race organisers in case of trouble, a satellite YB3 tracking system for sending our position once a day along with a short message, and finally, an AIS[25] receiver to be alerted to the presence of ships equipped with it (especially commercial vessels). A lot of communication equipment for a race supposed to be sailed the old-fashioned way!

My Rustler was heavy and slow, rather unpleasant to helm. It wallowed quickly, skidded cheerfully, requiring me to reduce the sail area as soon as the wind reached ten knots (Force 3). In short, I had my work cut out to tame this peculiar boat and, most importantly, make it fit to face the high latitudes of the Southern Indian, Atlantic and Pacific Oceans.

First decision: I hired Olivier Morice, who often worked for me, and together we removed the abundant teak on the deck to make the boat lighter, refastened the chainplates, checked every bolt, installed two watertight bulkheads at the bow and created a space in the bow to store my sails. From morning till night, amid ubiquitous polyester dust and a deafening racket, we continued our 'mass destruction' project. I wanted to make the cockpit locker watertight, install a new mast and engine, overhaul all the deck hardware (winches, pulleys, cleats, tackle, blocks) and adapt it to my way of sailing, just as I'd done on all my

---

25. *Automatic Identification System. System for identifying and tracking all equipped boats. This is especially important for the safety of solo sailors because an alarm goes off when a ship comes within a predetermined distance.*

previous racing boats.

The hundreds of thousands of visitors who gathered around the pontoons before the start of the eighth Vendée Globe in November 2016 couldn't miss my Rustler, prominently displayed in the technical area of Port Olona with its beautiful royal blue and white paint. It was quite a curiosity compared to the racing machines lined up nearby.

Once the race started, I'd have all the freedom to put my boat back in the water and carry out tests and training during the winter. I sold without difficulty, or rather, for a bargain, the original mast and old sails to a young couple who lived with their daughter on a steel boat, which reminded me of my youth. Later, I would find out that the new mast ordered at the maximum size allowed by the rules was too large and not suitable for such a circumnavigation.

At the same time, I planned to install first one and then two furlers for the genoa and staysail[26] – a first for me in a west-east circumnavigation on such a small boat. After all, I'd be 73 years old at the time of departure, and it might not be necessary to over-play the tough guy by having hank-on sails. I was trying to maximise weight savings aloft, minimise drag and not needlessly overload my boat. It's my rational and Cartesian[27] side, typical of a Maths teacher.

Based on my repeated experiences sailing around the world, I knew that attention to detail is key to success. I'd almost always prepared my boats alone or with a very small team, and I wasn't going to change my habits now. Despite

---

26. *Sails (jibs) of different sizes or sail areas.*
27. *After René Descartes, French mathematician and scholar.*

my easy-going demeanour, I'm very demanding with my suppliers, constantly negotiating prices to get the best deals. They've known me for a long time; know that I have no debts to anyone and that when I'm satisfied, I am very loyal.

I regularly visit the Tarot sail loft, where I ask them to cut and prepare nine sails. I needed to reassure myself, to make sure they wouldn't be too heavy because I had no doubts about their durability. Above all, I didn't boast to my future competitors about ordering a new mast that was 1.5 metres shorter. Even though I knew it would be a clear disadvantage in light winds, I didn't need to argue excessively to convince Michel Audouin from Sparcraft to design this compact rigging. After five circumnavigations on much more sporty and technical boats, sailing a 36-foot cruising boat solo didn't worry me too much.

The final winter before the departure, I 'sailed as much as possible', as the jargon goes. In essence, I got experience, but never alone. It was a matter of conviviality. When heading towards Ireland, where you're almost guaranteed to encounter strong winds, it was best to share the time with Lionel Régnier, my faithful assistant, or with two or three friends always ready to roll up their sleeves.

I was, of course, looking for a sponsor and would find one thanks to a long-time friend. A few years ago, executives from an insurance company contacted me: they wanted to celebrate the retirement of one of their highly esteemed executives, André Geffard, who was passionate about sailing. Would I be willing to give a lecture at the Musée National de la Marine (Navy Museum) in Paris for the occasion, and, to complete the gift, could he and his wife join me on a cruise on my Sun Odyssey 52.2, which was then based in Greece? André Geffard was so enthusiastic about the experience that he went further and, a year later, embarked on another week-long cruise, still in my company. We became friends.

Despite some promises that didn't materialise, I still hadn't found a sponsor for the upcoming race, I explained to André the ins and outs of this old-fashioned competition and left him a dossier, just in case.

A few months later, we met at the Salon Nautique International de Paris (Paris Boat Show) at the Porte de Versailles. There, almost casually, he dropped his bombshell: "Oh, by the way, Jean-Luc, I mentioned your project to Matmut[28]. They're on board!" I knew André had some connections. I discovered that he was the vice-president of this company. And then he added, "By the way, do you have a standard contract?" A few weeks later, I received a bundle of papers to initial and sign, followed by the first bank transfers. Luck was on my side once again, it's chance and friendship that have been my best allies. Conventional paths definitely aren't for me.

---

28. *Mutuelle Assurance des Travailleurs Mutualistes (MATMUT), insurance company.*

Chapter 6

From college to my first boat

I'd dreamt of it since my second internship at Les Glénans. I really liked the Corsaire, a cute little trailer-able 5.5-metre cruiser made of plywood, designed in 1954 by Jean-Jacques Herbulot[29] for the famous sailing school. This guy was a genius. He also designed the *Vaurien*, the Caravelle, the Mousquetaire and the Cap Horn – so many boats that greatly fuelled my passion.

And on top of that, what a competitor he was! He competed in the Olympic Games four times, finishing just off the podium in the Star class in 1932 in Los Angeles.

I got my first sailboat at the age of 21. I found a not-too-expensive, second-hand one in Le Havre with a trailer, except, I didn't have a car and so, took the train from Gare Saint-Lazare in Paris to get there.

In the absence of a better option, I put it in the water each time by pushing it by hand with the club's crane. Its name was *Gide*, a combination of Gi-nette and Dé-dé, its previous owners. In the ports I sailed to, the name had its effect with people taking me for an intellectual, an admirer

---

29. *One of the best known figures in the world of French sailing.*

of the great writer[30], which never failed to make me smile.

Personally, folding my tall frame into a space the size of a two-person Canadian tent didn't pose a problem for me. Nor did the facilities on board – two berths, the bow for storage, no kitchen and a bucket for a toilet – which were rather basic, to say the least. On such a small boat, bad weather catches up with you more quickly than on a larger vessel, but that didn't scare me. Quite the opposite!

What I loved more than anything was participating in regattas in the English Channel as the skipper of MY boat. I would even do my first solo race during the Semaine de la Baie de Seine (Bay of Seine Week).

I embarked on adventures with Nicole, my partner, whom I met while studying at Jussieu University. She was also a Maths teacher, and soon to be my wife and mother of our two children. I had been officially engaged twice before, but each time the relationships fell apart. This time, it was love at first sight. Out of caution and eager to start MY family, I decided to skip the 'engagement' stage.

Nicole didn't particularly like boats, but like many partners of sailors, she resigned herself and went along with it. To her credit, it must be admitted that the comfort of my 'nutshell' was far from that of a yacht. Nicole and I decided to get married very quickly, in 1967, less than a year after our first meeting. Our honeymoon didn't take long, of course, celebrated on board our Corsaire.

During a stopover in Courseulles-sur-Mer in Normandy,

---

30. *French author André Gide, winner of the 1947 Nobel Prize for Literature.*

we signed up for the Sunday regatta. The second place we secured was enough to make us happy. I was very proud of my crewmate. We got tossed around in the famous Raz Blanchard (Alderney Race), with its whirlpools and strong currents. Nicole took it in her stride, she was a good sport. And both of us loved stopping at Alderney, Sark, Jersey and finally Guernsey, where Victor Hugo liked to recharge.

Beyond this wonderful journey together, what mattered to me was building a loving and close-knit family, perhaps because I missed out on that aspect quite a bit. Even though, unlike my younger sister Dominique, a psychiatrist, I avoid endlessly dwelling on the past and constantly analysing the whys and wherefores, I unconsciously feel the need to fill a void in this area.

Then comes May 1968. I admit it: my next weekend along the Channel coast concerned me more than the events themselves. Furthermore, I had to urgently retake a physics exam. It was chaos, as General de Gaulle so aptly pointed out. Jussieu University in the fifth arrondissement was evacuated the day before, and access was blocked by some striking students. The riot police (CRS) were not far away.

Nevertheless, I managed to spot a gap in the fortress near the Jardin des Plantes (Botanical Gardens). I managed to sneak through and found the professor who was supposed to examine me amidst a mess of rubble and leaflets. She was so surprised to see me that we corrected my exam paper on the spot, with the excellent result you can imagine. I still chuckle about it.

Before that, I did indeed take part in a few protests.

How could one not be swayed by the speech and energy of someone like Daniel Cohn-Bendit?[31] But I remained pragmatic: my meagre teaching assistant salary was essential to me.

What's more pressing was that my wife's brother was seriously ill, on the verge of death. Since most nurses were on strike, we took turns to keep a vigil at the hospital – my wife, her sister, my father-in-law, my mother-in-law and myself. Since I had stored some petrol before the service stations ran out, I still had enough to transport them one by one on the luggage rack of my moped.

Paris was almost at a state of war, turned upside down, especially in the district where I was supposed be working. I came across heavily armed gendarmes (French paramilitary police) everywhere and had to show ID to enter Saint-Sulpice college in the sixth arrondissement, where I worked as a supervisor. I was giving some Maths classes, but towards the end of the year, they were often skipped.

However, the school, as the students used to say, was ahead of its time. There was a TV in every classroom, all connected to a central control room. The choice of videos was extensive. From student to supervisor to teacher, the circle was complete.

I really began my teaching career at Saint-Nicolas, on Rue de Vaugirard, a private technical education institution located nearby. Here, I taught Maths and Science to future electricians, mechanics and carpenters, and I enjoyed the

---

31. *Daniel Cohn-Bendit was a student leader during the unrest of May 1968. In 1994 he was elected to the European Parliament.*

diversity. The following year, I returned to Saint-Sulpice, and also taught part-time at the Cours Morin (Morin School). I mostly commuted through Paris on my moped and didn't count my hours. The unique aspect of this school was that it was exclusively attended by girls. The headmistress warned me, "Mr Van Den Heede, I must have someone reliable; you are the only man in the establishment!" My sessions were limited and scheduled at the end of the day. Fifteen minutes before the end of class, the students started talking and touching up their make-up.

I quickly found a solution: Just like in a football match, as soon as attention wandered, I stopped – and added the 'stoppage time' to the end of the session. The next time, it was so quiet you could hear a pin drop, and the class ended right on time. Such childish antics amused me, certainly more amusing than my military service that followed.

Of course, I requested to serve in the ranks of the French Navy. But hoping for that was like hoping for the moon: I ended up in the equipment division at Montluçon barracks, where I immediately felt like I was wasting my time. This dead-end was depressing, just like my comrades who knew nothing about the sea and limited their activities to three priorities: drinking beer, smoking Gauloises cigarettes and waiting for the '72', those three-day leave passes without which an ordinary soldier would go mad. I had my fair share of them like everyone else. And it was during one of these '72s' that Nicole and I conceived little Élisabeth.

At 24-years old, married and a soon-to-be father, I was entitled to a bit of respect: I became an accountant at the École Militaire (Military School), just steps away from the

Eiffel Tower. Now, I had office hours and almost always returned home in the evenings to be with Nicole, who was gradually rounding out. My paperwork job wasn't exciting or complicated. I was alone, as my colleague − a civilian − was frequently on sick leave. The director of the establishment where I worked was a retired general, and I found myself among other military personnel with desk jobs. It was a stark contrast to the maritime adventures I craved.

The school where I previously worked as an accountant needed a Maths teacher, and apparently, the director there had some high-level connections. One morning, the colonel summoned me. "Van Den Heede, I have a somewhat special request: Your former school is asking for your services for three and a half days a week. I have no objections, if you can fulfil your duties here." In addition to my meagre conscripted soldier's salary, I had a small income coming in. Some might say, not without reason, that I was in a cushy position. With my military service fulfilled, Nicole and I aspired to one thing: leaving Paris to get closer to the sea.

Just six months after Élisabeth was born, we took her on a Muscadet, a small 6.40-metre plywood sailing boat borrowed from a friend, for our first cruise to the Isles of Scilly, located off the southwest tip of England. We were not very attracted to the south of France. However, setting a course westward excited us.

I wrote to several private vocational high schools in Brittany and attached the excellent references I had earned from the three institutions where I started teaching. I didn't want to end up in a public high school somewhere between Thionville and Charleville-Mézières far from the sea. Also, my Parisian experience made me appreciate the atmosphere in vocational schools. Classes adapt to the trades the students are learning, and it's less monotonous than repeating the same thing four times to four classes of the same level.

I received a positive response from Lorient in Brittany. Not only did the school's administration offer me a full-time position, but they also informed me that they had a sailing club. A dream came true! However, to my surprise, most students didn't take advantage of this opportunity. So, I consoled myself with a few vacationers who were passionate about sailing. All my free time was dedicated to it and soon, the localities of Locmiquélic, Larmor-Plage, Port-Louis, the Coureaux of the Île de Groix, Belle-Île, Houat or Les Glénans had no secrets for me, just like my new sailboat, a Cap Horn named *Clampin*, which replaced *Gide* to accommodate Élisabeth. A few more trips and I would be able to name all the cardinal buoys that marked the bay, by their first name!

By chance, I learnt that the prison at Lorient-Ploemeur was looking for a teacher. Even though I already had a job, I volunteered for this second position, even though my background as a student and then a teacher in the private sector is not well regarded by GRETA, the consortium of institutions responsible for courses for prisoners. I was the 'black sheep' of the flock, and I know that my predecessor couldn't handle it, but regardless, I enjoyed the experience.

I knew nothing about my students, neither the reasons

for their incarceration nor the duration of their sentences. But they knew that if they were diligent, they could earn sentence reductions. A great motivation. I felt like I was being 'useful'.

There were strong-willed individuals, but also some great guys. One day, a young man approached me: "Sir, I didn't understand everything, but since I have 15 years to serve, I hope that will still be the case next year!"

I tried to offer them practical and fun exercises to engage them if not captivate them. And it worked; for example, I showed them how to generate electricity with a lemon, a galvanised nail and another made of copper – two electrodes of different metals. They caught on quickly and even asked if they could use this discovery beyond the inevitable lights-out limit. It was in my nature: I have always liked to help and charm and one doesn't go without the other. Gaining their respect was one thing, but it meant nothing if that authority wasn't accompanied by a little camaraderie.

I believe that the virtues of a good leader draw from all these contradictory and complementary elements at once. Even today, former students write to me. Mr 'Védéhache' appreciates this recognition and values the fact that they eventually learnt to spell my name correctly.

Chapter 7

The objective: 240 days

GOLDEN°GL⊙BE°RACE

Since I stopped teaching – over a quarter of a century ago – I've dedicated 100% of my time, or nearly so, to boats. I've had numerous experiences and exchanged ideas with many sailors. I know very well that a race is won in the preparation phase as well.

For this race, for example, my provisioning was the result of careful thought. On an Excel spreadsheet, I input the fundamental data. For each average speed, I calculated a total duration: 5 knots = 230 days; 5.02 knots = 229 days; 4.98 knots = 231 days, and so on. Given my previous voyages and my knowledge of the boat, I estimated an average speed slightly above 5 knots, which is a little over 9 kilometres per hour. Not wanting to run out of food, I added a buffer. Total: 240 days' worth of provisions.

The Maths teacher in me never changes. In everything, I try to calculate, anticipate and plan, even though experience shows that for every voyage, unforeseen events can sometimes disrupt predictions. A new spreadsheet detailed everything to bring on board, from vacuum-sealed bread to ready-made meals, from chocolate to desserts, from wipes to absorbent paper, not forgetting salt, olive oil and herbs de Provence. Almost casually, with 150 litres of diesel, 250 litres of fresh water in tanks, 50 litres of sparkling water, 60 litres of good wine, food, clothing, tools and spare parts, all this nice mess represents at least one ton of provisions to fit into a boat that already weighs almost eight tons.

I also prepared a passage plan with major waypoints – Cape Finisterre, the Canary Islands, the Equator, the Cape of Good Hope, Cape Leeuwin, Hobart, Cape Horn – and calculated, if everything goes roughly to plan, a total passage time of 220 days for a final distance of 26,434 nautical miles, which is approximately 49,000 kilometres. There was no doubt; this voyage was going to be long. On his ultra-modern giant multihull, in December 2017, François Gabart[32] completed his journey five times faster and in just a little over 42 days.

Numbers, always numbers. I consulted Jean-Yves Bernot, the famous meteorologist, to confirm that my planned route and the expected performance of *Matmut* would be consistent.

At the same time, I commissioned a climatological study of my southern route, which was relatively high in latitude – around 45 degrees – from Christian Dumard, another specialist in weather routing. This route was unlike my previous circumnavigations. This reinforced the forecasts from Jean-Yves, known as 'the wizard', and

---

32. *François Gabart is a French professional offshore racer who won the 2012/13 Vendée Globe, setting a new race record.*

my own convictions. With a bit of luck, by optimising my route, without major technical issues or weather surprises, I might even be able to complete my circumnavigation in 188 days, with an arrival in Les Sables scheduled for 4th January 2019, a result that would, I had no doubt, be the best of all scenarios.

We always learn from our mistakes. During the first Vendée Globe in 1989/90, there were 13 of us, all venturing into the unknown. Each of us had to grope our way through. I had based my calculations on the time it took Olivier de Kersauson[33] to circumnavigate the globe on his large trimaran *Un Autre Regard* a year earlier, which was 125 days. Since I was sailing on a monohull that was five metres shorter, I calculated that I needed at least 150 days of provisions. In reality, and to my surprise, I completed it 13 days faster. Yet, in a supreme paradox, after rounding Cape Horn, after 75 days at sea, I had almost no strength left because I hadn't eaten enough in the Southern Ocean.

Was this because I was afraid of perishing or was it the thrifty side of my nature? Rest assured: during the Atlantic ascent, I made up for it without counting. This time, there were no unpleasant surprises.

Unlike the Estonian Uku Randmaa[34], who was so short of provisions that he lost 25 kilos, I never had cause to complain. Every three days, I would swallow some vitamin supplements. Not as a precaution against scurvy, the

---

33. *Olivier de Kersauson – French sailor and double winner of the Jules Verne trophy*
34. *He completed the Race in third place.*

disease that decimated the crews of the great explorers in the 18th century, but simply to maintain my fitness. The only downside was losing a tenth of my red wine, which I probably shouldn't have brought in three-litre containers.

In the Southern Ocean, the cardboard boxes quickly became damp and disintegrated, and the plastic bags turned porous. Welcome the smell of vinegar mixed with mould and diesel! My daily 25 centilitre glass of wine wasn't always available, but fortunately, the aluminium pouches of Pomerol held up better. Apart from the first few days, I never cooked, satisfying myself with reheating hearty but tasty meals, a mix of canned and freeze-dried food. I had brought a lot of music for my vintage cassette player, about 50 tapes – a mix of rock, blues and classical music, including – no surprise – quite a bit of Pink Floyd, and supplemented my entertainment options with a series of audiobooks that were perfect for the long periods spent at the helm.

When I'm using the autopilot inside my cabin, another sound always obsesses me: the noise of my boat. The slightest creak of the hull, the smallest rope friction makes me pay attention. During my record-breaking run against the prevailing winds on board *Adrien*, which was much larger and faster than my current boat, 15 years ago already, I had planned to bring 15 books for 122 days. As I'm naturally cautious, I added 15 more. In the end, I only read about a dozen. To be honest, you're always busy on a boat, especially when it's devoid of electronics. You don't notice the time passing.

Normally, I do a lot of helming, especially downwind

and under the spinnaker. On *Matmut*, due to the lack of real enjoyment of sailing because she was so slow compared to what I am used to, I was less diligent. I admit and this boat wasn't very pleasant to 'drive'; being heavy and not very responsive and not planing easily. Fortunately, I had extended the tiller by doubling its length, which gave me much better leverage. I hadn't counted exactly, but out of my 5,000 hours of sailing, I think I was at the helm for only 700-800 hours and almost never at night.

Another time-consuming activity: I recorded all my sextant sights in my school notebooks. It was a tedious task imposed by the Race organisation under the threat of disqualification. In this age of constant connectivity, it might seem incomprehensible, but the Golden Globe Race was aiming to celebrate the spirit of the 1968 edition. That spirit sometimes came with unexpected gestures of kindness. Case in point, the telephone call – normally prohibited – with Odile during the mandatory weekly communication window. Knowing that everyone was listening, just like in the old days of Saint-Lys Radio[35], we kept the conversation to a few banalities: "How are you? Yes, I'm fine. And you?"

Nevertheless, this exchange did us both a world of good. It's often forgotten, but during these long solo races, loved ones left ashore suffer almost as much, if not more, than those at sea. Odile, my new partner whom I met after my separation from Nicole, entered my life in a boat-related

---

35. *It was a marine radio station that operated from 1948 to 1998, transferring radio calls from the open sea to telephones on land. Conversations were audible to everybody listening on the frequency.*

context, through a meeting that had its share of spice.

A few months after my first Vendée Globe, I was on the verge of selling my *36-15 Met* to Isabelle Autissier, who was preparing for the upcoming BOC Challenge[36]. We raced together offshore from Lorient in the company of the Quillery company, one of my sponsors, so they could get a feel for the boat.

During the final race on the Sunday, we languished for a few hours due to lack of wind, and the regatta was eventually cancelled. The skipper of a competing boat asked if I would take two girls back to the port. It was 'urgent' and they were determined to come on MY boat as a challenge. The impressive dimensions of the *36-15 Met*, and my modest fame, earned through my third place finish in the Vendée Globe, had its effect and we got to know each other. On land, the pleasantries continued over a few glasses of champagne as I signed my first book. In short, we exchanged phone numbers and I said I would be happy to meet them again sometime.

A while later, passing through Nantes, I called both numbers without even knowing who was who. One goes to voicemail, the other answers. It's Odile. Funny how things work out. Despite being a logical, maths-oriented person, I don't underestimate chance and randomness.

Not everything can be explained or calculated. For instance, I'm said to be insensitive to temperature variations. Never too hot, never too cold. Some kind of reptile. Go figure. In the morning, I can put on a fleece, but if later

---

36. *A solo around-the-world race with stopovers.*

in the day the temperature rises above 30 degrees, I'll not notice and keep it on me.

Conversely, at southern latitude, I can go out on deck in just a shirt without feeling the cold bite. That's probably why I have a bit of a reputation for being tough. I can't provide any precise explanation; it's just the way it is.

Even more surprisingly, there are times when I don't realise it's raining. This was particularly the case at the end of that round-the-world trip when I arrived in Les Sables. Was it due to the emotions of victory and reunions, my focussing on flying the spinnaker or the fear of being approached by one of the many spectator boats? Who knows? When I later saw the videos and photos, I was surprised to discover that it was pouring with rain!

Well, this quirk had one exception: For some time during the Golden Globe Race, I'd been suffering from dampness, especially in the southern latitudes. It was a vicious circle: I'd go into my wet sleeping bag, come out of it and the boat was fogged up. It was impossible to put on dry clothes, even impossible to dry them. Despite appearances, although I share some of the characteristics, I am not a polar bear. Throughout the Golden Globe Race, I cursed the infiltration of water inside my cabin and used who knows how many rolls of paper towels to prevent my table from becoming a permanent puddle.

The chart table looked like a bathroom. My efforts to keep it somewhat dry were without any success, of course. And I won't even mention those vicious breaking waves that, at times, when I had folded my cockpit cover above the companionway, took malicious pleasure in flooding everything inside. Even my original portholes were leaking, oozing water 24 hours a day. I had considered changing them at one point before the race started. I didn't and made the big mistake of only re-seating them with sealant.

Mark Slats[37], on the other hand, took his portholes off his boat and laminated fibreglass over the holes. His boat must have been dark inside, but it was effective against leaks and humidity.

During my five previous circumnavigations, I never brought any additional heating on board, and I didn't change that for the last one. Heat intensifies condensation inside the cabin, causing more dampness. Also, the temperature differences between the living area and the outside are detrimental. When you're cosy inside, you have even less desire to go outside. That's the paradox. And using an oil or gas heater involves carrying fuel, which adds weight to the boat. I've always been very careful about weight. During my first Mini Transat, my Muscadet was so light that it supposedly floated ten percent higher above the water.

All of this may seem like minor details, but the devil is in the detail. Here's another example: on land I timed the lifespan of a gas bottle and calculated that I would need a little more than two refills for the journey. Not wanting to eat cold meals and being the careful planner that I am, I set off with three bottles. The mathematician in me, you see. I'm not entirely sure if my competitors did the same.

---

37. *He finished second in the Race.*

Chapter 8

The other side of the horizon

During the first single-handed transatlantic race in 1960 – The OSTAR[38] – I discovered the character of Francis Chichester, a phenomenon who didn't fit the usual mould of offshore racer. This man left a deep impression on me. Despite my young age – I had just turned 15 – I followed his race and exploits closely, always on the lookout for newspaper clippings or another book about him.

A professional aviator, this true-blooded Brit, who was 'as blind as a bat', had enlisted in the Royal Air Force during World War II. He served valiantly and wrote a technical guide, a kind of tutorial, to help pilots with their 'on-the-fly' navigation. He was already 49 years old when he discovered sailing, and a decade older when he won the 1960 race between Plymouth in England and Newport, Rhode Island in the east coast of the United States.

On his famous *Gipsy Moth* series of yachts, he also completed a west-to-east circumnavigation in 1966/67 in 226 days with only one stop, becoming the second

---

38. *The Observer Single-Handed Transatlantic Race. It was a milestone in sailing as the first single-handed trans-ocean yacht race.*

sailor after the Argentine Vito Dumas to achieve this solo circumnavigation via the three Capes.

I am fascinated by both his simplicity and modesty. What's more, I am impressed by his ability to grasp the basics of offshore sailing in so few years. I also have a lot of appreciation for Herbert 'Blondie' Hasler, another competitor in this legendary race. A lieutenant colonel in the Royal Marines, he successfully led a raid against German ships while paddling up the Gironde River in a kayak in 1942. After this heroic act, Hasler dedicated himself entirely to yachting, notably developing the first self-steering gear that ultimately wasn't too dissimilar from what we will all be using for this round-the-world voyage.

Another discovery: Jean Lacombe, a brave and good-hearted last-place finisher in the OSTAR transatlantic race. A 44-year-old leatherworker, filmmaker and photographer crazy enough to set sail on a 6.50-metre Cap Horn designed by the inevitable Jean-Jacques Herbulot. Four years later, he would return to the helm of a Golif of the same size, finishing ninth out of 15 in the second edition of the OSTAR – a truly remarkable performance completely overshadowed by the victory of a young French naval officer named Éric Tabarly on *Pen Duick II*.

A few years later, I became the owner of a Cap Horn very similar to Jean Lacombe's. It was a good yardstick to measure the distance I had left to travel to possibly emulate my heroes.

It was at the 1977 Salon Nautique (Boat Show), held under the CNIT dome at La Défense, Paris that I learnt of an Englishman named Bob Salmon, who wanted to organise a 'mini' transatlantic race aboard 6.5-metre sailing boats. His idea was to counter the 'arms race' – the soaring costs and budgets of single-handed racing campaigns, exemplified by Alain Colas's famous *Club Méditerranée* – four masts, 1,000 square metres of sail, and 11 kilometres of electrical cable – an unsuccessful competitor in the OSTAR held a year earlier. These English people always seem ready to go in a different direction or take the opposite approach. Salmon didn't take long to come up with a name for his project: Welcome to the 'Mini Transat'.

I immediately embraced the commitment of this freelance journalist-photographer who contributed to financing the 1968/69 Golden Globe Challenge, which I have already talked about at length. Although it seemed far-fetched at the time, I found his idea rather brilliant, and I started thinking about my potential participation, perfectly matching my financial means at the time.

Well, 'means' is a stretch. I obviously didn't have a penny in my pocket, no sponsor, no 6.5-metre boat. Nobody knew who I was. My background – an unknown Maths teacher far from the sea with no notable achievements – wouldn't be of much help. Moreover, I had just taken a year of leave from the school where I taught to finish building my steel boat. Could I extend it for another quarter? I can only dream.

What if I tried my luck by going to see Victor Tonnerre, the renowned sailmaker from Lorient, known for cutting all the sails for Tabarly's *Pen Duick* boats? I knew Victor well. He was not always friendly, but he had an impressive network and didn't mind my company. Perhaps he could introduce me to André Aubin, the wood craftsman who builds Muscadets on the banks of the Loire? Playing matchmaker didn't bother him, and there we were at the Boat Show, heading towards the builder and his designer. When I asked Aubin to lend me a Muscadet to compete in the 'Mini', he was naturally sceptical. I pleaded my case, emphasised my experience in the Scilly Isles with my wife and my six-month-old daughter, and argued that this new challenge could make single-handed racing much more accessible.

Partially convinced, André Aubin introduced me to Philippe Harlé, the designer of the Muscadet and a collaborator from the very beginning. In his unmistakable high-pitched voice, he asked, "So, young man, why the Mini Transat?" In my stentorian voice, I presented my arguments: My love for small boats, the philosophy of this new race – that I believe in it – to make solo racing more accessible, the sporting fairness of the event because the boats are largely similar, and so on.

Did the partially deaf Harlé hear me? His reply is clear: "Young man, I like you!" Looking back, the exchange may have seemed trivial, but it was fundamental in my eyes, defining my journey and indicative of the loyal and friendly relationships I have always maintained with my supporters or suppliers. No need for long speeches, just a few truths, mutual trust and respect. Aubin was equally direct and pragmatic: "I will pay for the return trip of your boat by cargo if you finish in the top five overall and at the top of the five Muscadets entered." Deal! It was an unwritten contract sealed with a firm handshake. Additional motivation: Achieving results.

In my car on the way back, I was singing at the top of my voice as I left Paris. I was going to compete in my first transatlantic race, and it's a solo one to boot.

During the late winter and throughout the spring, I trained solo in all weather conditions. I decided to enter the 100 miles of the Concarneau, a solo race that qualifies for the Figaro race. The weather was dreadful, with storm-force winds and rough seas. Today, no organiser would start a race in such conditions. Out of the 30 or so participants, only three of us make it to the finish line. I win the race on corrected time ahead of Jean Le Cam, an 18-year-old Breton who sailed the family boat, an 8.55-metre Armagnac, also made of plywood, designed by Philippe Harlé and built by the Aubin shipyard, naturally.

I was exhausted, both literally and figuratively, but I thoroughly enjoyed myself. The third place finisher in the race was Alain Delord, who was rescued from his liferaft south of Tasmania in 2013 while attempting a solo circumnavigation, by none other than ... Don McIntyre. It's a small world.

During this challenging race, I thought about my childhood heroes. About Alain Gerbault, always facing epic storms, or Marcel Bardiaux, who didn't hesitate to beat to windward for long stretches. Immersed in solo sailing, I felt that I was getting closer to their convictions. I loved only having to rely on myself. Of course, I was not Chichester, Tabarly, Knox-Johnston or Moitessier, but there I was, ready to cross the 'big pond' for the first time, in a race and without anyone's help. I was 32 years old, with a wife and two children, Élisabeth, now seven years old, and Éric, four years old. I felt prepared, had complete confidence in myself on this borrowed boat that I now knew inside out. Honestly, even if it sounds conceited, I had no doubts.

In Penzance, Cornwall, on 8th October 1977, there were 26 competitors, including Bob Salmon, but also Halvard Mabire[39] and Bruno Peyron[40], 21 and 22 years old, respectively. The first stage, which took us to Santa Cruz on the island of Tenerife, didn't count in the race results, but served as a qualification before the big leap to the Caribbean and the island of Antigua. We could take our time and make one or two stops, as long as we arrived safely in the Canary Islands.

Off the coast of Portugal, we encountered a severe storm. I'd already faced very bad weather in a Muscadet and hunkered down. Even some cargo ships slowed down. Unfortunately, two participants were missing at the finish, Maurice Fouquet and Patrick Van God, lost at sea. I still remember Patrick's wife, waiting for her husband's return on the seawall of the port of Tenerife day after day, increasingly disheartened, before being confronted with the tragic reality.

Some of the media triggered a controversy saying these 6.5-metre boats, originally designed for coastal cruising,

---

39. *Halvard Mabire, pioneer of ocean racing and on the podium in 1977 in the very first edition of the Mini Transat.*
40. *Bruno Peyron broke the outright round-the-world sailing record in March 2005. He was the first winner of the Jules Verne Trophy in 1994, for completing a round-the-world trip in less than 80 days.*

were not fit to cross an ocean due to their small size.

I was about to discover what three weeks at sea alone in a 'nutshell', in which I couldn't stand upright, just sitting down, really mean. My boat may have been spartan, but it was sturdy and seaworthy above all else. A true baptism of fire awaited, accompanied by new fears, this time in the trade winds.

I didn't do too badly and finished fourth in the race, which was won by Daniel Gilard on *Petit Dauphin*. The piña colada offered at the finish tasted like paradise: I had fulfilled my contract. Not only was my loaned boat repatriated, but it was also displayed at the next boat show. Better yet, André Aubin hired me as a salesperson. I sold two Muscadets and an Armagnac and earned my small commission. It was a good deal, bolstered by the fact that I was convinced of my appetite for solo racing.

During those two years, alongside my sporting adventures, I had also been building a 12-metre steel ketch near Lorient. It was an amateur construction in a garden, a shed, a vacant lot in very 1968-spirit.

I designed it with very Cartesian measurements – 12 x 4 x 2 metres – drawing inspiration from the Finot Rêve d'Antilles plan and from *Pen Duick III* and its tulip-shaped bow. I built the structure myself, cut the frames and sheets, but subcontracted the welding to the Millet shipyard. My brother Philippe helped me finish the basic plywood interior, which was sufficient for cruising. I decided to name it *Euclid*, after the Greek mathematician. A way of revenge.

Do you remember *Gide* and my supposed admiration for literature? Let's not lie about it. There was no ambiguity with *Euclid*: I indeed love maths and I am a teacher on top of that.

On this boat, I first did some sailing training trips, then, following a misunderstanding about a house we bought, we decided to live aboard *Euclid*, while the house was being sorted out. My children enjoyed this somewhat bohemian life that we shared in the Lorient harbour. To add to the incongruity, after returning from the Mini Transat, I resumed my teaching position.

Chapter 9

Not without fear or blame

Am I afraid to die? I'm often asked that question. Clearly, no. However, I've experienced some significant fear at sea.

The first one was during the 1977 Mini Transat, during a night of a tremendous storm. I was still a beginner and had very little knowledge of meteorology.

Nevertheless, I hadn't realised that this cumulonimbus cloud formation – thunderclouds in layman's terms – which was developing vertically, feeding on the warm water of the trade winds, would turn into a real bomb.

I was completely overwhelmed by events. The gusts were so powerful that I felt like my one-ton sailing boat would take off like a feather swept away by the breath of a child. Lightning was streaking the sky and the thunder was deafening. It was a terrifying experience and it made me acutely aware of the power and unpredictable nature of the sea.

Despite these moments of fear, I never lost my passion for sailing. There's a special connection between sailors and the ocean, a deep respect for its forces, and a constant desire to conquer its challenges. It's a world where you must be vigilant, prepared and always ready to face the unexpected.

It's a world where fear can be a companion, but it's also a world where the rewards are immense, and the sense of freedom and adventure is unlike anything else.

Lightning streaked across an inky sky. I was convinced that it would strike my metal mast, obsessed by the memory of a sailing boat struck near Le Havre, which was not a pretty sight when it returned to port. I was in a panic. Despite being close to the age of Christ at his death, I knew that even prayer wouldn't have helped.

Sitting inside, my liferaft in its container like a suitcase on my lap, paralysed by fear, I waited for the storm to pass, simply grateful not to have been struck by lightning. After the race, the designer Philippe Harlé explained to me the differences in potential energy between clouds and the ground, or between neighbouring clouds. I then better understood the phenomenon.

The second close call I experienced was in 1990 during my first Vendée Globe, when I found myself navigating in the middle of a field of icebergs. At that time, competitors were free to choose any imaginable route, even the southern-most, very close to Antarctica and therefore closer to the ice. To make matters worse, we didn't have satellites dedicated to the tracking and observation of drift ice. It was a matter of luck. Take an orange and spin your finger around it. The closer you get to one of its 'poles', the less distance you must travel to go around it. That was my motto.

One beautiful morning, I was busy on the boat's foredeck and spotted ice chunks barely larger than those you'd typically use to chill your pastis. I returned to the helm, convinced I had been dreaming; was it merely the crests of a few waves frothed by the foam? A new mirage, or so I thought. Then I noticed a surprising cloud to my left, almost sitting on the sea. A few seconds of hesitation, and I convinced myself it was an iceberg, a massive one, a gigantic thing. I felt unease rising within me, but at the same time, a certain disbelief, as if this vision, marvellous in a way – it was the first time I tasted the experience – couldn't possibly end in catastrophe.

In broad daylight, perhaps, the obstacle could be avoided or circumvented. But at night? And what about all the little growlers, those chunks – big enough to pierce a hull – that break off the monster, unexpected, imperceptible amid the wave crests? At that moment, my heading is clear: I had set a final route, skirting the Antarctic continent. I was sailing at 61 degrees 50 minutes south. The cold was absolute, and the water temperature was close to zero. The deck was covered in frost, and small stalactites formed under the spreaders.

It was against reason, but it was the competitive drive that had taken me into those perilous waters. I couldn't bring myself to let Titouan Lamazou lead the way. I kept one eye open and tried to navigate through that treacherous area. At dawn, the same nightmare vision, and the same white spots as the day before. I was sailing downwind, and it was fast. This time, it was a minefield combined with a dead end, as if I was entering an intoxicatingly beautiful bay, but surrounded by hostile mountains.

Now, the enchanting impressions and aesthetic feelings were over; it was fear knocking at my door for real. To slow down the boat, I immediately reduced sail area and headed upwind. On both port and starboard sides, I discovered dozens of blocks, sometimes reaching 30 metres across in size, with hallucinatory shapes and colours. I had to find a way out.

I succeeded and notified Titouan on the HF radio, according to our usual practice. He was much higher, at 58 degrees south. Unlike him, I didn't have radar on board *36-15 Met.* Kindly, he gave me the positions of the icebergs he encountered, forcing me to be even more cautious. It was decided, even if it meant losing time, I was heading back up, and quickly!

Hearing Titouan's sing-song southwest France accent was so comforting. The ordeal wasn't over, but I felt a burden had been lifted. Then began an endless watch, punctuated by wave after wave of stress. I watched the sea crashing against the menacing icebergs all around, just like it would on ordinary cliffs. The slightest collision and I would be lost. No radar, no sophisticated means of communication, but no engine either! For this inaugural race, freedom is the rule. It's undoubtedly a good thing to have, but it has its limits.

I didn't have a choice; it was a matter of survival. For 24, 36, 48 hours, I fought sleep to continue my course to the northeast. Time seemed endless. When the autopilot was steering the boat, I didn't take my eyes off the horizon, startled at the slightest sound from the hull. Whatever am I doing here?

Clinging to my teak tiller, I kept nodding off and after two days and as many nights, I couldn't take it anymore and regularly dozed off. The fear in my gut did not leave me until, finally, the pieces of ice were no longer big enough to pose a threat to the boat.

During the Golden Globe Race, I didn't experience such fear. Race rules played a role in that. Competitors are not allowed to go below the 50th parallel, except when heading down from around the 40th to Cape Horn jutting out down to 56 degrees south. But I would be lying if I didn't mention that despite this, apprehension always lurks. That's the nature of sailing in those regions. Nothing is guaranteed. The unexpected always has a say. When the sea is rough, with seven, eight, nine-metre waves crashing against the hull, I wonder every time if the boat is going to stay in one piece.

This perpetual introspection becomes almost obsessive. The risk, the uncertainty, it's always there, inexorably linked to solo sailing in the open sea. It's this element of the unknown that makes the magic and terror of these solo races around the world. Each day brings its share of unpredictable challenges.

Contrary to the impression given, I am not made of wood or stainless steel. Only time and experience round off the edges a bit and make one more philosophical, more fatalistic. When sailing my previous boats, especially the 60-footers, I would attach myself to the lifeline, armed with my harness and its sturdy tether. But on my Rustler, that was very rare, even in bad weather. I would tell myself that in these seas – the 'largest desert in the world', as Kersauson put it – alone, far from everything, it's of no use. Whatever will be, will be.

However, I do always keep in mind to hold on. Firmly.

When I move on all fours, I always have one hand on the boat. Before every manoeuvre, I visualise the task I'm about to do, and constantly think about how I will approach it. I also consider what might happen if a wave broke at that moment or if I lost balance due to an unexpected gust of wind. I anticipate. To better prepare for the moment, I even talk to myself out loud: "If you take the boom brake off, you need to be careful in case the boat gybes unexpectedly", "watch out, there are tricky waves that could unbalance you", "be cautious about this repair, it would be better to rather position myself to windward".

This 'intellectual routine' always considers the fact that I could potentially end up in the water. Just like that, in a fraction of a second. I think about it constantly when I'm on deck. During this last circumnavigation, I chose to steer very little when conditions became dangerous. Considering how physically demanding steering is, I prefer not to be exposed to the elements.

On this type of boat, we were constantly at the mercy of the elements. It hardly ever surfs, and when a breaking wave came from behind, it could lift the hull and hurl it into the next wave or it could pour onto the deck. That was the biggest danger compared to much lighter racing sailboats that accelerate down the waves before catching the next one. I let the wind vane self-steering system handle it, which, in strong winds, steered the boat quite well even if the course varied by 20 degrees from side to side. My hydro wind vane self-steering system worked well. I was thrilled with it. It was a self-contained device that didn't operate the tiller, and therefore the boat's rudder, but had its own blade rudder for steering.

When the blade was adjusted – and the boat changed course – through a system of gears, by an aerial appendage with a sail that aligned itself with the wind. It's also because my boat was originally equipped with this device, and the race organiser is a fan of it, that I chose it.

Many of my competitors, who had self-steering gears to adjust the tiller with a system of lines attached to it, experienced repeated difficulties. Every day, I was grateful for my choice. During downwind gales, I closed everything – the sprayhood and the companionway hatch, and I stayed inside, letting the boat go about its own business.

Chapter 10

Seven months without setting foot on land

GOLDEN°GL⊃BE°RACE

It's time to cast off the lines. The last days on land are quite exhausting, with demands from all directions – information briefings, final checks, meetings with journalists, visits from friends and family, my children and grandchildren, my sisters and my brother. The usual anxiety before departure seizes me, but I don't show it, reinforcing my reputation as a tough guy and the associated monikers such as 'man of iron' or 'hermit'.

A major regional newspaper drives the point home: 'VDH: the old man and the sea.' My white beard and my venerable age make the comparison easy, and suddenly I'm elevated to the level of the famous hero from Ernest Hemingway.

To be honest, I find all this amusing. Over the years, I've grown accustomed to it. People like me, and I like people. There's a connection, and my infectious laughter adds to the mix. Am I relaxed, though? Not entirely. The start of a race is just that – a race. There's the pleasure, the satisfaction, but there's also stress, doubt, erratic sleep –

everything that comes with that unique moment when, in every sense of the word, you dive in.

This is my sixth circumnavigation. In theory, I know what to expect. But at the same time, I've never done such a long journey. The distance is the same, but it is going to take much longer.

No one is immune to last-minute issues. Shortly before departure, a France Télévisions' crew joins me for one final report. I lose focus for a moment and that's when a foil windsurfer skims past close to the stern of my boat and rips off my log. Of course, I don't realise it right away, only when the same madman, still zooming by, tosses the cordage and its small propeller onto the deck. The problem is that the log is now missing. I am beside myself because this mechanical log not only measures the distance travelled, but also provides the speed. When navigating without GPS, both distance travelled and speed – along with heading from a compass – are essential in working up a dead reckoning position on a chart to compare with a position fixed from a sextant sight.

Lionel, my assistant, had spent ages sourcing it and, thanks to a friend, I had five propellers specially made just in case they got eaten by a fish.

I search the internet to see if I can find another one. No luck. I'll have to make do with the Walker, my backup log. Moitessier had the same log, which lasted throughout his entire journey, even though he lost nine propellers in the end.

For this log, I only have one spare propeller, and there's no time to make more. So, as a precaution, and with the organiser's approval, I secure it with a Spectra line made of a high-tech fibre – just in case a new windsurfer passes by. As it turns out, this proved to be a blessing: Four months later, during my dismasting, this unbreakable five-millimetre line allowed me to make makeshift repairs and, in the process, save my circumnavigation.

Caution and precaution. Patience and perseverance. You need to stock up on these before considering orbiting the planet. 20 years ago, when I contemplated breaking the record for a solo circumnavigation against the prevailing winds and currents (east to west), I knew from the get-go, more or less, how long it would take – between 120 and 140 days at sea. It seemed quite daunting, but that didn't stop me from attempting it three times previously – and failing each time.

In 1999, the hull delaminated. In 2001, the keel gave way. In 2002, it was the mast that broke. To achieve my goal and improve Philippe Monnet's record, it took me 122 days. For this new retro-style circumnavigation, I knew it would take 100 days or more, and for a good reason, my boat is almost 15 metres shorter.

I made my decision knowingly, with the right mix of recklessness and selfishness. As often before my departure, those around me show more concern than I feel myself. Since I live in Les Sables-d'Olonne, when I return home each day, I inevitably meet neighbours in the elevator lobby. They are lovely, caring, but they must think I'm a gentle madman. I try to put on a brave face, make jokes, act relaxed.

The same goes for my competitors. Most of them are

heading into the unknown. Not me. I know that the first days of the race will be crucial, especially psychologically. You must set the pace, not let yourself fall behind, but also conserve energy. I'm here to finish and win at the end of the race, not just at the beginning.

Despite having the utmost confidence in Lionel, my assistant to whom I delegate many things, I inspect and check every detail. When you go solo and non-stop, you can't rely on chance. Forgetting a simple lighter, or a rescue mirror or a pair of scissors can ruin everything. I remember that during the first Vendée Globe, Jean-François Coste, who was skippering Éric Tabarly's *Pen Duick III*, renamed *Cacharel* for the occasion, simply forgot his roll of nautical charts at his hotel. Fortunately, he realised it a few minutes after the start.

In the realm of clothing, what to pack is crucial. There's no skimping on spare clothing, fleece, hats, gloves. In all areas, I tend to be generous, but I'm less obsessed than some people: Chris Dickson, during a Whitbread (crewed round-the-world race), insisted that his crew members sacrifice the handles of their toothbrushes, and Lawrie Smith, in the same race, allowed only one pair of boots per crew member, even requiring that they cut them up to turn them into sandals once they reached more temperate latitudes.

The atmosphere at Port Olona, where the 18 competitors in The GGR are moored, is friendly. The summer season is in full swing, it feels like a vacation, and whole families stroll along the race pontoon. Although I'm quite popular with the kids, I sign fewer autographs than Kylian Mbappé, who would win a football World Cup in Russia a few weeks later, but I still hold my own quite well. Each to their own competition.

On 14th June, we all sailed from Les Sables to Falmouth for a festive send-off. That's where Robin Knox-Johnston had set sail exactly 50 years ago. A well-deserved tribute to this exceptional sailor before heading back to Les Sables d'Olonne, where the real starting gun would be fired on 1st July.

I often cross paths with my friend Philippe Péché, known as 'Pépèche'. To me, he's my most serious competitor. While he hasn't done much solo sailing, at 57, he has a lot of sea miles under his belt, sailing with Tabarly, Gautier, Desjoyeaux, Le Cléac'h, and competed in the America's Cup. For this double winner of the Jules Verne Trophy[41], the Golden Globe Race is a turning point. A Breton living in Australia, he says he wants to 'complete the circle'. I also know his father, Jean-Paul, a renowned sailor who lives near Lorient.

In our circles, it's hard to keep a secret for long. Back when I was scouring ports in England in search of my Rustler, I had randomly crossed paths with him. His half-smile gave it away: He understood that, like his son, I was planning to race in the GGR. Naturally, our searches overlapped. Eight days apart, we visited the same boat. In the end, the Péché family acquired a boat in poor condition but secured a generous sponsor to refurbish the vessel – PRB – which had been involved in sailing for a quarter of a century. There's no doubt that 'Pépèche' is not here to

---

41. On Bruno Peyron's catamaran, Orange.

just make up the numbers. His real challenge? Endure a hermit's life for seven months on what he calls a 'clothes iron' (referring to the hull shape of the Rustler 36) – not easy when you've been racing for the past 10 or 20 years on ultra-sophisticated, rocket-fast sailing machines, with some of the best sailors in the world

As the days go by on the GGR pontoon in Les Sables d'Olonne, I find myself inspired by the diversity of sailors and boats in this competition. Each one has their own unique story and motivations, making this race a celebration of individual spirit and adventure.

Australian Kevin Farebrother, 50 years old, sails a Tradewind 35. He's a firefighter in Perth, more of a mountaineer than a sailor. He has already climbed Everest three times. But he won't stay in the race for long: after just two weeks, he throws in the towel and lands in Lanzarote, saying he 'can't stand the solitude'. I must admit, I'm a bit surprised. Without delay, he would sell his boat and head back to the Himalayas to conquer his fourth Everest.

Nabil Amra, 42 years old, is Palestinian. Born in the United States, he works as a stockbroker in Minnesota. He discovered sailing only five years ago but, after reading Moitessier's *The Long Way*, it took him just a few minutes to officially enter the GGR. Nabil is a bit quirky, but incredibly friendly and filled with conviction. Not only does he want to honour his father, a former lieutenant in the US Navy, but he also aims to highlight that Palestinians living on the coast in Gaza, are denied access to the sea by Israel: "The greatest sailors from my country are trapped in Gaza, and I want to raise their flag." However, he wouldn't go very far; plagued by autopilot problems, he dropped out after 17 days at sea at the Canary Islands.

Antoine Cousot, 47 years old, and Loïc Lepage, 63 years old, are the other French competitors. Both have travelled extensively as professional yacht delivery captains and have been inspired by the stories of their predecessors. Antoine's ketch, *Métier Intérim*, with its apple green hull, is hard to miss. It's a Biscay 36 built in 1975, completely refurbished. Loïc chose a Nicholson 32 MK XI designed by Peter, the youngest son of the famous naval architect Charles Nicholson. *Laaland*, the smallest boat in the fleet, measures 'only ten metres, but the design's reputation for robustness is well established.

I particularly like the story of Abhilash Tomy. A commander and pilot in the Indian Navy, he has already completed a non-stop circumnavigation from Mumbai and is considered a legend in his country, despite India's limited sailing tradition. At 40 years old, Abhilash decided to embark on this solo journey to test his skills and endurance once again, and I have immense respect for his determination and spirit.

Abhilash's boat is a replica of *Suhaili*, the ketch that Robin Knox-Johnston sailed 50 years ago, and which he built himself in India. However, Abhilash's *Thuriya*, is constructed with a modern wood-epoxy and composite technique. With this bold choice as a tribute to the first winner, Abhilash perfectly embodies the spirit of the Golden Globe Race.

Finally, I have a soft spot for the British sailor, Susie Goodall, 29 years old, the youngest sailor and only woman in the race. A sailing instructor, she has been immersed in the world of sailing since a young age and is sailing on *DHL Starlight*, another Rustler 36. She could be my granddaughter.

Rustlers are the majority in the fleet, with a total of six on the starting line, all similar, except for mine with its slightly shorter mast. I feel reassured about my choice, even though I briefly considered the Gaia 36. Only the Finnish sailor Tapio Lehtinen opted for this faster boat on paper, but perhaps also too heavily loaded, hence low in the water.

On 1st July, it's time to go. No more checking inventories and equipment. The weather is splendid, the wind light and the swell gentle. It's the height of summer. On the big Les Sables beach, you can see more towels than sand. After a sluggish start, we must tack into the wind.

A sailing boat cannot sail directly into the wind. Getting from A to B, you often must sail twice the distance – and it may take three times as long as going directly from A to B. In summary, we must zigzag from one point to another, lengthening both the route and the time.

The exit from the Bay of Biscay is challenging and not very enjoyable. In light winds, I am slightly handicapped compared to my competitors with taller masts, and therefore more horsepower in their sail 'engine'.

Two days after the start, I cross paths with a cargo ship, the *Forban*, which gives me my first position. Generally, to avoid getting into endless discussions about 'I'm racing old-school without modern positioning methods, etc.', I simply mention that my GPS is out of order and then note my position in latitude and longitude, which I compare with my

The start of my singing. I am 6 years old

With my maternal grandmother aged 8

With my maternal grandfather aged 10

My mother, always very distinguished

In Berck, shrimp fishing.

On a moped in 1962 … and without a helmet!

My first internship at Glénans aged 18

I am the team's goalkeeper (third from right at the top)

In the forest with my children Élisabeth and Eric

With Sir Robin Knox-Johnston's book in Falmouth in 2018 – the 50th anniversary of his voyage starting

Many of the skippers and Sir Robin at the Royal Cornwall Yacht Club before the start of the race
Standing, left to right: 2 from RCYC, Mark Mark Slats (partially hidden), Jean-Luc Van Den Heede, Mark Sinclair, Sir Robin Knox-Johnston, Antoine Cousot, Uku Randmaa, Tapio Lehtinen, Susie Goodall, Philippe Péché
Sitting, left to right: Igor Zaretskiy, Istvan Kopar, Nabil Amra, Are Wiig, Loïc Lepage

Matmut in the parade of entrants to the Golden Globe Race 2018/19 in Falmouth

Matmut with other Golden Globe competitors in Falmouth in 2018

The solid wood navigation desk on the boat where I spent 211 days

My first meal on land after my victory with Odile, my partner, and Lionel, my assistant

Permanent concentration in the southern seas during the Golden Globe Race

Arriving at the Pontoon des Sables d'Olonne, and the joy of victory!

My valiant Rustler 36 on the morning of arriving off the coast of Vendée

dead reckoning. Occasionally, this saves me from tedious sextant calculations. There is intense maritime traffic north of Spain, along the cargo shipping routes.

On my SHOM (French Hydrographic Office) chart, which still smells new, I make sure to stay away from the TSS (Traffic Separation Scheme) marked in pink on the map. It's like a highway for commercial vessels. On 4th July, a German ship I ask about its position immediately responds, "That's funny, someone else just asked me the same question." It turns out it was Mark Slats, who, like me, wanted to verify his positions because there is no GPS on board.

If his dead reckoning is correct. He's ahead of me. I quickly realise this 42-year-old Dutchman, born in Darwin, Australia, and four years younger than my son, is going to be a serious competitor. He's a real powerhouse. He's nearly a head taller than me and weighs at least 120 kilos – mostly pure muscle. I feel like a lightweight despite my 1.87 metres and 90 kilos. A former kickboxing champion, he used his winnings to buy a 46-foot sailboat and has already sailed solo around the world – well, almost, as he sailed with his dog onboard.

Mark, who secured a good sponsor – Ohpen – somewhat late in the day through a chance encounter, has a team manager and a large support team. His boat, like mine, is a Rustler 36, older but with more sail area. In Les Sables-d'Olonne, when I observed his boat, I quickly realised it had the profile of a potential winner.

GPS technology has been in existence during both Mark's and Philippe's entire lives, so they had to learn about celestial navigation and how to use a sextant. They took a course before the race, whereas I've been familiar with this instrument for over 45 years as a sailing school instructor. However, I still did a little refresher with an expert.

Chapter 11

The Bardiaux effect

Ever since I devoured his book *Aux 4 vents de l'aventure*[42] in 1958, he has been my absolute idol. His personality left a mark on me; his example influenced some of my life choices. I was only 13 years old when I first heard of him, and I instantly identified with him.

Marcel Bardiaux was born far from the sea, in Clermont-Ferrand, a working-class city in Auvergne and the home of Michelin tyre factories. Bereft of his father, who was killed a few days before the armistice of World War I, and his mother, who was unable to raise him alone, he ended up in an orphanage at the age of eight. From his unhappy childhood, he inherited a fierce determination and boundless energy.

---

42. The story of Bardiaux's circumnavigation was published in two books: Aux 4 vents de l'aventure: Le defi au Cap Horn *and* Aux 4 vents de l'aventure: Par le chemin des écoliers. *The first book – covering his passage from France to Tahiti – was translated into English as* 4 Winds of Adventure *and published by Adlard Coles Limited in 1961. Unfortunately, the second book was never translated into English.*

Nothing stopped him, not even building a boat on his own in the middle of a war, or transporting the ballast material for his boat in a cart attached to his bicycle. Bardiaux was also an indefatigable globetrotter. His boat not only allowed him to cross oceans but also enabled him to meet people from diverse cultures, and to explore unknown worlds. What he wanted was to travel, see the world and meet others.

His life made me dream, as I returned to my grandparents' or parents' every evening with no real chance of escaping. I imagined myself discovering the world in the way he did.

What I also admired about him was his determination. He set a goal, and he achieved it. He didn't go where the wind took him like many others but to the places he decided to go, no matter what it took. The fact that he travelled solo fascinated his hosts at each stop, adding to the reception or hospitality he received. Bardiaux often took advantage of this.

In 1950, five years after the end of World War II, during which he was taken prisoner, escaped and was recaptured, he embarked on a circumnavigation. And what a voyage – eight years of sailing, with a total of over 300 stops.

In my eyes, Bardiaux represents a kind of marine Superman, a true character from a novel, tough as nails.

He was ill-tempered, rugged, with unwavering physical endurance. When he sailed around Cape Horn against the prevailing winds (from east to west) in the heart of the southern winter, the feat seemed astounding to me. He was not afraid to sail like this for a week if necessary. Ultimately, only one thing stopped him: a pretty woman with a delicate figure or a fresh smile, and I don't mind that either!

His rustic wooden monohull measured 9.38 metres and was named *Les 4 Vents* (*The Four Winds*). Either he was a masochist, crazy or a bit of both. He continued his journey seemingly unfazed, filled his cruising kitty by taking on a multitude of odd jobs, had fun and then left. Previously, he had also completed a tour of Europe of nearly 25,000 nautical miles (46,300 kilometres) on a rowing canoe and adopted the ancient Eskimo rolling technique once developed by the Inuits.

Truly, this guy was priceless.

I was 14 years old and discovering the Salon Nautique (Boat Show) for the first time situated, as it was then, on the banks of the Seine. By the water's edge, the spectacle was magical. I felt like the sea was coming to me. I strolled alone amidst the boats set out on the grass. I contemplated a *Vaurien* and then a Requin, a wooden hull with perfectly drawn lines. But that was not all: I discovered a small 5.5-metre sailing boat named Corsaire, with two berths, even more attractive. That's when I first became captivated by this lovely cruiser with its glossy varnish. I already pictured myself hoisting the anchor and setting off to explore distant shores. I envied these exhibitors with sun-kissed skin and rough hands who, when not in their workshops, test their boats on the water whenever necessary.

Three years later, due to its success, the Show would move and set up at the Palais des Expositions of the Centre National des Industries et Techniques in La Défense (CNIT), just a stone's throw from my family's home. Every January, the Show was a tradition for me. I climbed the hill to the esplanade where this gigantic reinforced concrete vault of over 22,000 square metres stood, inaugurated by General de Gaulle.

That morning, I noticed a disciplined line stretching out from a table covered with books and a man diligently signing them one after the other. Marcel Bardiaux in person! He was just as I imagined him, rather handsome with his bull-like neck, toned muscles and a gaze that's both clear and determined. Of course, I already owned his book but it was at home. I immediately left the exhibition hall, negotiated with the ticket collectors the possibility of re-entry and jumped on my bike. I was so excited that I felt like I was racing in a Tour de France time trial. I stuffed the book into a bag and pedalled the few kilometres that separated me from La Défense.

Finally, it was my turn. I handed over my book as if offering a sacred sacrament. My mentor, my master, raised an eyebrow, appraised me and, to my great surprise, grumbled the unthinkable: "Sorry, kid, I only sign books that I sell, not the ones people bring to me!" Crash! Defeated, betrayed, I turned around, slowly enough to hear him make matters worse: "But if you join the Friends of Marcel Bardiaux Association for two years, you'll receive my newsletter every quarter ... and then I'll sign your book!"

I knew the great solo sailor who claims to have taught Moitessier everything, but at that moment, I also discovered a perfect little money-making apothecary. I was disappointed but not discouraged. I did the maths, gathered my few Francs, rejoined the queue, and left with my copy, properly signed. After all, I didn't care if he was known to be venal, Pétainist, egocentric and in permanent revolt against the whole world. A few months later, when I received his newsletter, all was forgiven.

I immersed myself in its information. It's filled with valuable technical advice and tips for solo and cruising navigation. I would later realise how influential this newsletter would be for me.

Many years later, I mentioned Bardiaux to Odile, my partner. At the time, he lived alone in Nantes on the Erdre River aboard *Inox*, a sturdy 15-metre monohull built from stainless steel, hence the name. It was a fortress that lived up to its name, transformed into a bookstore and overflowing with books, which he sold as much as he could. While she was jogging along the riverbank, she came across this boat I've talked so much about. There was a small sign: 'To see me, ring here!' She introduced herself, said who she was, that we had common friends in Newport. Bardiaux invited her on board, offered her a drink, and gave her a signed book dedicated to his numerous conquests wherever he dropped anchor. When she left, he added, "The one who's waiting for you is very lucky."

I discovered another aspect of his character and his sexual exploits, which are quite spicy. I continued to diligently follow his final maritime exploits, sometimes adventurous, until his death at the venerable age of 89, after a global journey of nearly 400,000 miles that took him to all the seas of the world. A year before he met Odile, he had completed his 40th solo Atlantic crossing, just for the fun of it.

At the age of 84, in the middle of winter, he sailed

his boat from Halifax, Nova Scotia to Brittany, facing a terrible storm with winds exceeding 70 knots. During a manoeuvre, he was thrown into the sea but miraculously managed to grab a line and climb back on board. After 33 days of turmoil, he finally reached land. To think that at the age of eight, doctors had given him up for dead. I recall those photos of him in sleeveless sweaters, doing pull-ups or hanging from the shrouds as part of his daily exercise routine. I have sometimes been compared to him, albeit with less of a temper. What is certain is that I cannot help but notice many similarities between us, such as our strong penchant for circumnavigations on robust and austere boats. Our inclination to be warrior-monks.

This comparison doesn't bother me at all; on the contrary, I embrace it. I'm also fine with being called 'Mr Everyman' or a 'normal' person because I am. I might have a bit more determination than some, but above all, I'm fortunate to be optimistic and in good health, two priceless gifts from heaven. Often, I wonder if it doesn't stem from my early life difficulties. But I also confess to being reasonably 'serious'. I drink little, don't smoke and engage in sports. In addition to cycling, I used to play a lot of football and then tennis before my knees stopped me. In tennis, I compensated for my unorthodox style with a fierce desire to win every point until the last. But who can tell, there are healthy people who succumb to a heart attack or die of cancer. Life isn't very fair in that regard. Clearly, I've been dealt a good hand.

Chapter 12

Settling into a routine

GOLDEN°GL⊃BE°RACE

At the start of the race, we don't exchange much information among competitors. We have a scheduled radio check-in time set by race control. We compare our positions, chat in English and make small talk.

As for the weather, so far, I've had more than enough fair weather. There's so little wind that I, like everyone else, am forced to use the engine. Philippe and Mark are a bit ahead of me, but not far. I jot down in my logbook: 'Spent the night at the helm. Speed below 4 knots. IT'S DRIVING ME CRAZY!!!' To make matters worse, I tear my spinnaker slightly while bringing it back onto the deck. I'm annoyed with myself, but it is an easily repairable mistake. In the first few days, lacking reference points because we don't have GPS, I sometimes spend ten hours straight at the helm before collapsing. I reduce the sail, and then go to bed.

Surprise: the next day, I realise that I've covered 75 miles while the boat was controlled by the self-steering gear, which is more than the miles I covered the previous night while I was glued to the helm, steering by hand. It's quite discouraging, but the lesson is worth learning.

My typical day during the Atlantic descent is unchanging. I wake up with the lark and the sun. I do a full round of the boat to check if anything unexpected happened during the night. Then I have my breakfast: Tea, six LU biscuits (Lefèvre Utile, a French brand of confectionary) and canned butter.

During the 211 days of my circumnavigation, I never deviated from the essential 'breakfast' rule, except on the day of arrival.

Afterwards, if the wind is favourable and I'm flying the spinnaker, I can grab my cap and take the helm. If the sky is clear with no heavy clouds, a 'sextant operation' is necessary around noon. Again, it involves a precise process. First, aim at the sun, then determine my position by adding the zenith distance and the declination of the celestial body. For longitude, I typically do this about one and a half to two hours before solar noon. When the sun is higher and rising rapidly, three-quarters of an hour is sufficient. Sextants are highly precise instruments, but they are extremely fragile. They need to be handled with care. In fact, they are often stored in wooden boxes like jewellery.

While the water heats in the kettle to rehydrate my freeze-dried meal, I often take two or three more sightings to achieve an even more precise result. After performing my calculations, noting my position in my logbook and on the chart, I take a nap of about half an hour. Consistently, I lie down on the windward bunk, secured by a carefully stretched anti-roll canvas to prevent me from rolling off and ending up in the middle of the cabin.

The days pass quickly. Cleaning, tinkering, organising, I'm rarely idle but never rushed. On a boat as slow as this, there's no need for panic. A little more, and I'd be living in slow motion. Even when I prepare my meal and have lunch, nothing really constrains me, nothing compels me to watch the clock. After my nap, I even take the time to air out the often-damp mattress of my bunk. I don't have a set 'checklist', but I conscientiously check everything on and under the deck, from the mast to the sails, from the self-steering to the engine. I don't talk to my boat, but I do talk to myself, yes. Sometimes I scold myself when I mess up a manoeuvre when I lose balance. "Come on, VDH, hold on!"

Sailing downwind, a genoa is usually poled out to the opposite side of the mainsail to catch the wind more efficiently. A gybe under a polled-out genoa involves moving the long, aluminium pole attached horizontally to the mast, to the other side. It is a manoeuvre that takes time – almost half an hour minimum – but, depending on the state of the sea, it can also turn into a balancing act.

The final ritual: Before nightfall, at sunset, I have dinner, always taking my time. The three meals are what truly structure my day. Then, just before 'lights out', I always tidy up the cockpit, often littered with ropes and lines that resemble a tangle of giant noodles. It's best to clear the deck and create a clear manoeuvring space; at night, it's never good to trip over anything. A final glance at the compass, illuminated in red on its wooden frame, and then off to bed.

I don't put on pyjamas, of course, but I never sleep in my foul weather gear. The mattress and sleeping bag are already damp enough as it is. I hang my headlamp nearby and fall asleep quickly. If the weather is bad, and if I need to stay dressed – boots and oilskins – to be able to take action quickly on deck, then I lie down on the floor in the cabin, on top of the sail bags and spinnakers. It's certainly not a five-star bed, but at least I'm secure without the risk of tumbling through the cabin.

When it's essential for me to wake up, I set my old mechanical Jaz alarm clock – the blue Alpine one – for an hour and a half ... but most of the time I wake up before it rings. It's just as well because it would wake the dead. Automatically, I check if the course is normal, grab the sturdy wooden handrails of the companionway stairs, climb the three steep steps to the cockpit, then take a look at the wind vane, the sails and the mast. A quick survey of the sea conditions if it's rough and, when everything's okay, I lie back down for another 60 to 90 minutes of sleep.

It's crucial to regularly check the course. When the wind shifts direction, the boat follows the shift, because the vane on the self-steering gear is set relative to the wind direction.

I photocopied all the charts and Bernard Moitessier's daily positions from the first Golden Globe in 1968/69 and pasted them on the last pages of my logbook. This allows me to track my progress compared to his day-by-day progress. Despite the age difference, our boats have remained close in performance. It's very reassuring, knowing that Bernard was pushing *Joshua* to 100%, I'm sure of that, and not forgetting that *Joshua* was four feet longer than my *Matmut* (40 feet versus 36 feet), so I think I'm doing pretty well.

In a small blue notebook prepared before the race, I

compare all of this to my anticipated averages, for example, 11 days to reach Lanzarote in the Canary Islands. I'm on schedule, even if I must schedule a forced slowdown of an one and a half hours to transmit a Super 8 film and a roll of 24 × 36 photos to the race committee and, even at the last minute, participate in a brief 'live' interview.

It's mandatory for all competitors.[43]

I round the Canaries in third place, a few hours after Philippe Péché. Surprised, I learn that he has mistaken one of the islands in the archipelago, and his lead of 40 miles has evaporated. Now he's forced to backtrack and get back onto the right course. It's proof that you should never give up.

Mark Slats has also slowed down. He didn't choose the wrong island, but it takes him a long time to locate the buoy set by the organisers. I'm a competitor: Regardless of my opponents' setbacks, I charge ahead. I was a bit behind, but these mistakes made by my two rivals allow me to reduce my deficit. In a race, there are no small gains, only opportunities.

Every day, I compare my position to Moitessier's 50

---

43. *Because of the 'no modern technology' philosophy of the GGR, competitors have no means of transmitting photos and videos, taken while underway. They must make compulsory, timed, stops during the Race to hand it over to Race Control. Competitors are also required to do an interview – usually live – with GGR officials. No assistance in any form can be given to competitors during these stops. During GGR 2018, the stops were at Lanzarote (Canary Islands) and at Storm Bay (Tasmania).*

years earlier. He's faster than me. At the beginning of his circumnavigation, supported by ideal weather, he covered the miles with a hearty appetite. It only took him ten days to reach Lanzarote.

Bernard was maybe a bit dreamy, but he was also a seriously motivated sailor. I crossed paths with him on two or three occasions and remember a tasty anecdote. Well, tasty is a bit of a stretch.

Always a bit frugal with his expenses, before his circumnavigation, while preparing his provisions, he had written to a dog food manufacturer to ask about buying 150 cans of their best product. The company responded that, even though it was of good quality, the products were not intended for human consumption.

Apparently, Moitessier didn't care; this mixture wouldn't have posed any problem for him.

He also brought along large bags of rice, a staple in his native Indochina, plenty of instant coffee and dark tobacco for his cigarettes, which he rolled by pinching the tobacco between his toes. All things considered, I much prefer my cooked meals: green curry with chicken and coconut, veal scallops in Madeira jus, wild boar with cranberries, duck tagine, beef carbonade with beer or even rabbit. I've certainly become more refined with age, but I admit I had my fill of eating freeze-dried meals during my previous circumnavigations. There is no need to restrain my epicurean inclination any further. I'm adamant! Enjoying your meals when you're alone at sea is crucial for morale. And never mind if Bernard liked dog food and if Robin Knox-Johnston nearly poisoned himself with spoiled corned beef that he had taken in industrial quantities (216 cans).

Past Lanzarote, the wind gains strength, and the waves find their purpose again. Even better, the trade winds, which establish themselves at over 30 knots, are robust. I'm flying! I've rarely seen it like this in this season. I'm even forced to reduce my mainsail area and roll up my genoa. Maybe I'm not heading west enough, but I'm consistently covering over 160 miles a day. No reason to complain.

At the latitude of Cape Verde, the sun disappears. I keep my fleece on even though it's the middle of July. The water, like a river overflowing its banks, floods the side decks before rushing into the cockpit.

Sometimes, a flying fish lands on the deck, flapping its wings, but it's rare. Apart from the relatively mild ambient temperature and the warmth of the sea spray reminiscent of a thalasso jet shower, it feels like I'm in the Courreaux de Groix off Lorient.

This Rustler 36 is truly a peculiar boat. It struggles to exceed six knots and quickly drops to five knots even when the wind is weak. Only when sailing on a reach does it unleash its full power. Under those conditions, I sometimes average seven knots. On the other hand, when the wind dies down, and I'm forced to use the engine, I don't go faster than three to four knots. My arms hurt, I'm bored, and it's a nightmare.

My journal reflects my mood: '11pm. Fed up with the engine! Still no wind. I hoist the gennaker and go to sleep! 5am, still not a breath of air. Log in the morning: 1,117.5 miles when I was at 1,116 the night before. No comment!'

I am at 12 degrees north and still far from the doldrums[44]. Besides the calm spells, the real nuisance is the sargassum – massive, filamentous algae, that look like clumps of grass floating on the surface, and which, in recent years, have increased worryingly. Is it due to ocean pollution and climate change? I tend to think so, even though I don't have the knowledge to judge.

When you trail the log behind your boat – a surprisingly precise instrument – it's frustrating to constantly encounter these nuisances. They are visible to the naked eye, but given the length of the strands, they are impossible to avoid.

It's unbearable. I've never seen as much of them as during this circumnavigation.

Even though the sunrise on the horizon may resemble a Monet painting, I can't muster any enthusiasm. A chat with a ham radio operator informs me that I'm within a stone's throw of the two boats ahead of me. At least I didn't suffer for no reason. My real fear is having to get into the water to get rid of the algae that are slowing me down. It's happened to me before. In 1979, during my second Mini Transat, stuck in the middle of the Atlantic, I decided to inspect my hull. Not a breath of air and 5,000 metres deep. The water was tempting. Suddenly, as I was splashing around – I'm no Johnny Weissmuller – I saw a shadow forming nearby. I imagined it to be a shark that would, at best, tear off a leg or bite off an arm. I quickly surfaced, heart pounding at 200 beats per minute and knees half-bloodied. Rather than

---

44. *The Intertropical Convergence Zone (ICTZ), known for its calm spells and violent thunderstorms, on either side of the equator.*

the shadow of a shark, I had probably been frightened by the reflection of a sail. Nevertheless, it served as a lesson. If I ever have to work on the hull in an inaccessible area of the boat, I now have a TPS Cotten survival suit, and an inflatable beach dinghy bought at a supermarket. Two precautions that turned out to be unnecessary on that occasion.

After checking, I realise that, with my feet wedged in the lifelines and my body stretched out, I can reattach a pin on the wind vane paddle. Sure, the exercise is exhausting, it strains my thighs and stresses my lower back, but it saves me from taking a dip.

I pass through the doldrums as if it's a joke. It's as if they decided to remove them this year. However, I realise that both 100-watt solar panels are out of service. I'm angry because they're brand new. I think to myself that if, by any chance, I have a problem in the south with my hydro generator, I'm in trouble. But some good news briefly makes me forget all that: On 1st August, I learn that after a month of racing, I've just taken the lead. Yahoo! This is what I came for.

Chapter 13

The roaring Oceans – Indian & Pacific

GOLDEN°GL⊃BE°RACE

Solitude is starting to weigh on me. It's not the fact that I'm at sea; I obviously love that. I chose my way of life and I embrace it. When I embarked on this new challenge, I knew it would be long, very long. No, what weighs on me is the almost complete lack of contact with the other competitors. The fleet is spread out over 5,500 miles (nearly 10,000 kilometres). It's hard to believe.

The memories of my BOC Challenge and Vendée Globe are so different. My days were marked by daily radio check-ins with fellow competitors that reassured us, entertained us and kept us informed. Here, nothing, or nearly nothing. I'm too far from my rivals to hope to reach them via my SSB radio, and since satellite phones are prohibited, all I have left is the network of ham radio operators.

It's a world of its own. There are nearly three million of them worldwide and 13,000 of them in France alone. Since the first Vendée Globe, Claude has been tracking me whenever I'm at sea. He is assisted by Jean-Pierre, and I also know that Michel in New Caledonia might take over. But

I would like everyone to benefit from the weather updates. So, at my request, Jean-François will simultaneously create the 'Terre et Mer' (Land and Sea) association, which will find contacts worldwide to provide us with Navareas, the official weather forecasts that each country is supposed to broadcast on marine bands.

Ham radio operators are not amateurs at all – at least not technically. They practise their activity selflessly just for the pleasure of it. They are often benevolent tech enthusiasts, rarely sailors, holding a licence that grants them a call sign – like FK8IK, F6AKP, F1EDG, CT7ANH. During this Golden Globe Race, they are our only link to the world of the landlubbers, alongside the race HQ. Unfortunately, due to some abuse (the weather bulletin becoming too detailed and personalised), the use of ham radio operators will likely be prohibited in the next edition of the race. The initial intention was good, though.

We talk every day and, just hearing the voice, I know its Christian calling from Portugal or Jean-Pierre from France. The codes and procedures are always the same, '73', for example, means that your interlocutor is sending their regards. It's always very friendly. They often have the edge over the race HQ, which only provides a mandatory check-in once a week. That's how I learn about the dismasting in the Indian Ocean of the Norwegian sailor Are Wiig, who manages to make it back to Cape Town under jury rigging. Abhilash Tomy and Gregor McGuckin, who are competing for third place, also endure a severe storm on 21st September, the 84th day of the race with 70 knot winds and 15 metre waves. Both are battered by breaking waves and dismasted about 1,900 miles southwest of Australia. During his capsize, Abhilash, an officer in the Indian Navy and not really a novice, suffers a serious back injury. His message to the race management is quite concerning: "Capsized 360 degrees. Dismasted. Severe injury. Can't get up."

The red alert is triggered, and the MRCC (Maritime Rescue Coordination Centre) responsible for maritime rescues in that area is notified. The closest competitors are also called upon to assist in his rescue. The Irish sailor Gregor McGuckin's Biscay 36, located 90 miles southwest of Abhilash, is also without a mast, but Gregor is able to start the engine and change course to try to reach the shipwrecked Abhilash.

I learn that a French patrol boat, the *Osiris*, located 123 miles away, is also attempting to locate Abhilash. But the sea is dreadful, and it's only moving at four knots. An Indian military aircraft takes off from Mauritius and flies over the damaged sailboat. The rigging hangs down along the hull. The immobilised skipper inside turns on and off his distress beacon to send a recognition signal.

At least we are convinced he is alive. I lack details and confirmation, but perhaps it's better this way. I will learn later that two other aircraft will take off from Perth and La Réunion to meet the two shipwrecked sailors, and that the frigate *HMAS Ballarat* will sail from Fremantle and, finally, the Indian Navy will divert several other ships. Successfully transferred to the *Osiris*, the two sailors will eventually be disembarked at Amsterdam, a small island in the TAAF (French Southern and Antarctic Lands) located 800 miles northeast of the Kerguelen Islands, to receive initial medical care. They are saved!

In a different context, another ham radio operator I talked to during my first BOC race informs me that the American Istvan Kopar (who would finish fourth in the race) supplied water to a solo sailor who had run out of reserves while he was 3,000 miles from Perth. Fortunately, the solidarity among seafarers is still very much alive.

My fear before the start of the race was encountering severe weather. While on modern 60-foot IMOCA boats or maxi-trimarans, you can often avoid the worst storms by having enough speed to evade or even outpace them; on these older boats, there's no escape. I've verified this, and when I see the number of capsizes, dismastings and abandonments that have made headlines during the race, I'm reminded of Norman Jewison's famous film *Rollerball* from 1975, depicting a rather anxiety-inducing elimination competition.

Then, it is Loïc Lepage's turn to lose his mast, still in the Indian Ocean, still southwest of Perth in Australia. He, who wants to fulfil his dream of circumnavigating the world by sailing boat, is now forced to continue his journey on a 175,000-ton Japanese freighter bound for Buenos Aires. A bit later, on the 157th day at sea, it is the quiet Englishwoman Susie Goodall, in fourth place, who loses control of her boat in a severe storm. Hailing from Falmouth, where it all began, she is sailing an identical boat to mine but hers has a taller mast. Despite her limited experience in open waters, her start in the race was remarkable. I admire her determination and ambition. She reminds me of Englishwomen like Tracy Edwards, Ellen MacArthur or Samantha Davies, incredible women of talent, energy and achievement.

Just four hours before her violent capsize, Susie had concerns: "There's 60 knots of wind, and I'm taking hits; I really wonder what I'm doing here!" This is a question that all sailors ask themselves at one point or another. Yes, what am I doing here when I could be with family, cycling, watching a movie or having a good night's sleep? At 74 years old, I confess I still haven't found the answer.

"Dismasted. Hull okay. My boat nosedived and did a somersault. I was thrown into the cabin and lost both spinnaker poles. Nothing left to rig up a makeshift mast. The boat is devastated. All I have left is the hull!" Susie's distress signal is unequivocal. Even though she has secured her boat and didn't explicitly request assistance, it will be necessary sooner or later to initiate a search for her. The storm intensifies. The sailor can only arm herself with patience. She will eventually be hoisted onto the *MV Tian Fu* cargo ship registered in Hong Kong on 7th December.

That could have happened to me. I can't stop thinking about it. I believe I am the only boat whose masthead has gone well into the water and is still in the race. I must thank my lucky stars. Susie has disembarked in Punta Arenas at the edge of the Strait of Magellan, where her mother and older brother await. Setting foot on land, she declares right away that she will return to the Golden Globe Race. I am astonished but aware that one should never give up.

Chapter 14

Lucky stars

According to the Larousse dictionary, 'luck is a favour of fate, the fortunate outcome of something, the favourable situation of someone.' That definition suits me well. Good fortune has often smiled upon me. But I must also clarify that I meet two essential ancillary conditions: One, I firmly believe in luck, and two, I have a sense that I can provoke it. An example? We were in 1988, on the eve of my first Vendée Globe Challenge. I embarked on building *Éclipse*, a 60-foot aluminium yacht designed by Philippe Harlé and his partner Alain Mortain. To reach the shipyard located in Condé-sur-Noireau, it took about three and a half hours by road from Lorient. It was winter. The road was wet, even icy. I don't like driving in these conditions, but I had an important meeting that morning with the Garcia brothers, the contractors, and I had no choice.

As I reached the top of a hill, in the fading light, I lost control of my Opel station wagon on a patch of black ice and skidded just as a heavy truck was coming from the opposite direction. I counter steered, narrowly missing the behemoth and ended up in the ditch. I was safe and sound.

My maternal grandmother convinced me a long time

ago that the guardian angel does exist. On that day, at least, it was on duty.

I've met more than one person questioning my repeated strokes of luck, probably a little jealous of my success and zest for life. Personally, it fits me like a glove. After my first BOC Challenge on *Let's Go* in 1987, I returned on a delivery trip from Newport with my faithful friends Jean Lagüe and Eugène Doussal. After sailing around the world, this crossing of the North Atlantic in the middle of summer and with three of us on board was a piece of cake. We were even three days ahead of the welcome festivities planned in Locmiquélic, a small port overlooking the bay of Lorient, so we decided to go for a little impromptu pre-pilgrimage to the Glénan Islands, where it all began.

This archipelago, where the water is as clear as that of a Polynesian lagoon, left a lasting mark on me. It's where I sailed my first miles on a liveaboard sailing boat. The problem was that I realised that I didn't have any detailed charts of the area. The BOC route went through Cape Town, and then we headed for Sydney and Rio, but not through the Glénan Islands!

Venturing with a racing boat that's certainly narrow – 2.55 metres – but has a draft of 1.95 metres in an area filled with rocks is just plain reckless. Imagine my loved ones and all my friends finding out that after completing a circumnavigation, we grounded *Let's Go* and 'crushed crabs' just before the celebration. With heavy hearts, we decided to continue our journey but a few hours later, we spotted what looked like a nautical chart floating on the water. It was one. Unbelievably, it was a chart of the Glénan Islands, reference

7252. It was a French Hydrographic Office (SHOM) chart, type L, which doesn't tear or fade, even when completely soaked. You might think I'm embellishing or exaggerating, but ask my friends and family. I've experienced these twists of fate and I've never had reason to complain.

My crowning achievement and my claim to miraculous luck came during my BOC Challenge in 1994. I had just crossed the Bass Strait between Australia and Tasmania. It was a treacherous place, scattered with reefs and rocky islets. One must always be vigilant. The Indian Ocean crossing from South Africa was fast paced. I had to dig deep into my reserves to keep up with the leaders, especially Christophe Auguin and his *Groupe Sceta*. The sailor from Granville was flying like a bullet having just covered 350.9 nautical miles in 24 hours – a new record for a solo monohull – and he was heading for victory in the Cape Town-Sydney leg.

This last stretch to reach Sydney was upwind. To better shelter myself from the strong currents heading south, I decided to hug the Australian coast. I only had 50 miles left to cover, but I was getting worse and worse in the scorching heat. In the cockpit, under the autopilot, I rested my head on my arm, elbow on a winch and dozed off. For how long, I don't know. What I do know, however, is that my *Vendée Entreprises* was actually running aground on a white sandy beach. No, I'm wasn't dreaming. To think that just a few miles earlier or later, I would have smashed into the cliffs. Lying on its side, tossed by the waves, I assessed the situation. I was both furious and embarrassed.

News of my beachside interlude spread quickly. American Mark Schrader, the race director, chartered a helicopter and flew over me, asking me to abandon my boat. I refused. I was unable to make any diagnosis regarding damage to my hull, but there was no way I was not going to try something. Dozens of tourists approached the boat. I felt like the star attraction at a fair.

In all my misfortune, I found a new lifeline: I had run aground just a few miles from a port city – Port Kembla – which entitled me to outside assistance without being penalised.[45] A surfer threw me a line connected to a powerful local police boat that came to my aid. My boat shuddered, moved ... but the towline broke!

There were more and more onlookers on the beach. I heaved an old mooring line in their direction so they could try to pivot my hull perpendicular to the waves. The authorities' boat tried again with a thicker rope and a gentler pull. The beached 'whale' finally deigned to float on the water. The inspection that followed was not reassuring. My mainsail was in tatters; my boomkin – a small mast at the rear – was broken. The bilges had turned into a sandbox, but fortunately not too damaged. Against all odds, I'd saved my boat. A human chain formed and several support teams offered their assistance. Lionel Péan, who was preparing for the famous Sydney-Hobart crewed race, lent me a spare mainsail that volunteer riggers adapted to fit my mast. I managed to reach Sydney in the race, finishing second in the leg.

The stopover was certainly a scene of extensive work,

---

45. *The rules stipulated that you could be assisted without being penalised if you were less than 10 miles from a port.*

but I was going to set off again for Punta del Este on an almost new boat. In just a few days, the nightmare turned into a fairy tale. Luck can be cultivated. Perhaps that's why I never hesitate to lend a hand when needed.

I remember the first of my six solo circumnavigations in 1986 when I received a radio call from a Finnish competitor during a radio check with the race headquarters. He was complaining of a serious arm infection and the absence of suitable medication on board. His name was Penti Salmi and he was racing in my category, Class II. Concerned, I offered to change my course to assist him.

While we were close to each other, we had difficulty communicating. He didn't speak French and I didn't speak Finnish.

Since his English was approximate, and a drawing is often clearer than a long conversation, I sacrificed a postcard of a beautiful Brazilian woman showing her generous backside, taped above my chart table. I clearly drew where he should administer the injection and bundled everything – syringe, antibiotics and postcard – into a waterproof bag and threw it onto the deck of his boat. Nine days later, he had regained the use of his arm. At the stopover, he didn't have strong enough words to thank me, even though I never saw my postcard again.

Luck, mutual assistance and exchange is all part of my basic vocabulary. Another example? In 2002, as I was preparing *Adrien*, my new boat, and I needed two essential engines for it. I tried my luck with Pascal Jamet, the head of Volvo Penta France, without expecting much. To my surprise, he agreed to provide me with the engines almost instantly. Out of generosity or because he liked me? It's much simpler than that. It was because he, too, believed in good intentions, even the most trivial ones.

"Do you remember my son Romain?" he asked me. I admitted I was drawing a blank. Pascal Jamet got more specific: "A kid who, before your second Vendée Globe in 1992, sent you two Opinel knives in the mail for you to take around the world, one for you and one for him?" I remembered it perfectly. The knives, the letter and the padded envelope. After the race, which I finished in second place behind Alain Gautier, I did as he asked and sent the young boy back his 'around-the-world' Opinel knife. I even recall adding a card where I mentioned that my own Opinel had helped me cut sausage during my third rounding of Cape Horn. No doubt about it: luck can be cultivated.

Chapter 15

A strange stopover

GOLDEN°GLƆBE°RACE

Just like in the Canary Islands a few months earlier, the organisers of the Golden Globe Race require competitors to make a stop in Storm Bay, near Hobart in Tasmania. Of course, there's no question of setting foot on land or being resupplied, but for a brief period, competitors are free to engage in some communication exercises (quick interviews, photo file uploads, etc.).

Sailing along the south coast of Tasmania towards this mandatory meeting point is a real ordeal. It's impossible to close my eyes or even relax for a moment.

The area is treacherous, dotted with countless rocks and disrupted by conflicting currents. It's a playground for experienced sailors, much like the local hero, the much-loved Errol Flynn, a wonderful actor and seducer who jokingly admitted that 'sailboats were the only true wives [he] ever really loved throughout [his] existence.'

Landing in these parts with just a sextant as your aid is anything but a breeze. The swells of the Southern Ocean are often capricious, not ideal for precisely aiming at the horizon. A wave often bedevils your sun shot, so you need to repeat the operation several times.

Finally, I spot the Maatsuyker lighthouse. It doesn't move and allows me to confirm my previously uncertain calculations. Built on a 910-metre-high islet, it commands respect, just like the surrounding scenery, a succession of rocky teeth thrusting into the sea haphazardly. The most imposing one, located a few miles further north on De Witt Island, rises over a kilometre high.

Now reassured about my position, I set course for Whale Head. To make my way back to Hobart, I hesitate to take the D'Entrecasteaux Channel. This very French name belongs to an admiral who went in search of the La Pérouse expedition. Astonishing coincidence: I'm currently reading about the adventures of this sailor sent by King Louis XVI to map the uncharted regions of the Pacific Ocean.

Since my adolescence, reading has never left me: it is an escape and inspiration, I couldn't do without it, at sea or on land, I always have a book at hand and I admit that it often revolves around boats, journeys and adventurous destinations, but not always.

After some thought, I convince myself not to pass through the famous channel. Too risky. In case of adverse winds, this poorly marked place could turn into a nightmare. However, my obstacle course is far from over. Studying my detailed map, I think that passing between Tasman Head and The Friars would be a good idea. Certainly, the risks are not zero, but my gambler's instinct urges me on. No regrets, the sight is a marvel, perhaps the most beautiful I have had the privilege to admire during this circumnavigation. An unforgettable panorama. A generous, muscular, regular swell, crashing waves onto cliffs with phenomenal noise and power. Furthermore, and I can almost believe I'm near the Port Coton needles on the wild coast of Belle-Île, off the coast of Brittany.

The bottleneck is no more than 100 metres wide, but I still enjoy the situation, without trembling or panicking. And yet, afterwards, I learn that some friends who were tracking my route on the official race tracker momentarily believed that I had indeed run aground on the rocks.

Just as I entered Storm Bay, the wind drops and the light fades into night. Today, the 'Bay of Storms' doesn't live up to its name. There's not a breath of air, nothing, just the hum of my engine disturbing the nocturnal silence. I'm crawling along at four knots amidst several aquaculture farms, each one an unpredictable trap. With my engine purring and no wind, I'm at the helm, of course. The air is cool and my Peruvian-style hat once again proves very useful. A true charm, this headgear given to me by Don McIntyre in 1986, has accompanied me on all my circumnavigations.

At daybreak, I spot a rigid inflatable boat approaching. It's Lionel, my shore crew, and his companion coming to meet me. The end of the bay and the beautiful beach that marks it are not far off. Everyone is there: Don, Jane, Christophe Favreau, the photographer, Aida who provides commentary for the French followers of the race. The rules stipulate that I must moor to a buoy, alone, for a minimum of an hour and a half. With my gaff in hand, you might think I'm here for a picnic. These reunions abruptly break my journey of solitude.

My feelings are mixed, strange, but not unpleasant. The change in the situation is certainly incongruous. Just a few hours ago, I had nothing to envy, a solitary monk at sea shut away in my cell and, in an instant, I find myself in a video conference in front of a diverse audience gathered in a hall at the fishing school in Les Sables-d'Olonne, 20,000 kilometres away.

In the crowd, I can make out my partner, my big sister and my friends. Odile is wearing the nice sweater I gave her quite some time ago. I point it out to her, but there is a delay on the satellite and she doesn't understand. I repeat myself and our voices overlap and everyone laughs. I admit, the ridiculousness of the exchange is quite surreal, but it reflects the situation. It's like a solitary sailor, cut off from the world for weeks, suddenly reconnecting with the realities of the modern life.

To process all these emotions, I allow myself a short hour of sleep. Strangely, I can't seem to drop off. Perhaps it's the excitement of these friendly exchanges, both welcome and disturbing. No need to persist, I give up on my bunk and check my rigging, my mast, my halyards and my shrouds. Reassured, I cast off under sail and admire this paradise for one last time, a place where I'd gladly return for a leisurely cruise. It's not easy to break away from it. I spend the afternoon and the following night tacking. Finally, I return to my solitary routine. Southward bound.

Prudence dictates that I should pass well offshore of New Zealand, just as Bernard Moitessier did in his time. I remember well his account in *The Long Way*, filled with doubts and dolphins that came to keep his boat away from the coast. I find myself in a similar situation, except my gambler's inclination catches up with me once again.

What if, instead of following the same route, I cross the Foveaux Strait that separates New Zealand from Stewart Island, the very place where Yves Parlier played Robinson Crusoe during the 2000 Vendée Globe, rebuilding his mast alone and subsisting on dried seaweed? Since my first training at Les Glénans, I've always loved taking the shortest route through rocky areas. It's a matter of principle: you always gain by shortening your route. In this case, it would save me about ten miles, which is not insignificant. And the little dose of adrenaline I get as a bonus isn't unpleasant either.

Luck is on my side: a passing cargo ship confirms my position precisely. I remain vigilant, never leaving the helm, but under the light of a beautiful moon, my final apprehensions vanish. Of all the competitors in the Golden Globe Race, I will be the only one to navigate this treacherous passage. A perfect warm-up before swallowing the infinite Pacific, the longest part of my passage around the world, closed, mysterious and ending at Cape Horn, which we always approach 'on tiptoe' and with respect and humility.

Along the way, I'm surprised to see very few albatrosses, fewer than usual. Perhaps it's because I am sailing much higher in latitude? Maybe it's because it's winter during the nesting period? The albatross is an extraordinary bird that has always fascinated me. Even though I've observed its flight thousands of times, I wonder how it all works. It's a fantastic glider that can ride upwind and use the waves to its advantage. Watching them in action is a spectacle I never tire of.

It's not surprising that Manfred Curry, in his book *The Aerodynamics of Sailing*, a true bible published in 1925, draws an analogy between albatross wings and racing sails. I remember, during my previous circumnavigations, days with not a breath of air on a glassy sea, spending my time tossing bits of cheese to albatrosses that were also becalmed. Together, we spent hours waiting for the wind to help us continue our journey.

The take-off phase of an albatross resembles a comedy movie. Given their weight and wingspan, it takes them long seconds to lift off from the surface of the sea. They look like fire-fighting planes struggling to take off just after filling their tanks. I love it. It's a ballet that's both impressive and majestic, and it always reminds of the wonderful poem by Charles Baudelaire, which I learnt by heart, like all schoolchildren in France. I don't know if the poet sailed in the Forties – I doubt it – but for a few verses, I feel like he said it all, at least in the context of his time.

In the past, albatrosses were not universally loved; they were hunted and sometimes eaten. Today, I don't know a sailor who isn't fascinated by the purity of their flight.

A few days later, Don calls me on the satellite phone. I sense his concern. He informs me about a massive depression just ahead of me near the Chatham Islands and strongly advises me to let it pass. Not to tempt fate. For the first time since the start of the race, I voluntarily slow down (with a heavy heart) for about 12 hours. I think I've escaped the worst and convince myself of it. Not for long …

The Albatross

Sometimes for sport the men of loafing crews
Snare the great albatrosses of the deep,
The indolent companions of their cruise
As through the bitter vastitudes they sweep.

Scarce have they fished aboard these airy kings
When helpless on such unaccustomed floors,
They piteously droop their huge white wings
And trail them at their sides like drifting oars.

How comical, how ugly, and how meek
Appears this soarer of celestial snows!
One, with his pipe, teases the golden beak,
One, limping, mocks the cripple as he goes.

The Poet, like this monarch of the clouds,
Despising archers, rides the storm elate.
But, stranded on the earth to jeering crowds,
The great wings of the giant baulk his gait.

Roy Campbell, *Poems of Baudelaire*
(New York: Pantheon Books, 1952)

Chapter 16

Confessions & convictions, part 1

From a very young age, I've always had a strong competitive spirit. I don't really like the famous maxim – which I don't even think is his – by Baron Pierre de Coubertin[46]: 'The most important thing is to participate ...' When I played soccer, it was to win. Stopping a shot in the top corner and making my team win meant more to me than anything. I never take part in a competition if I have no chance of winning. I understand that others may do so, but it's not my thing. What's the point of playing a tennis match against Nadal just to watch the balls go by?

The five solo circumnavigations I've done in races – I'm not talking about my record against the prevailing winds – I hoped to win them. As much as when I'm cruising, I'll reduce sail before sitting down to eat, in a race, I transform into a racing beast. Every second counts. For example, if you decide to wait ten minutes before hoisting the spinnaker because you feel you're not quite awake or because you prefer to finish the chapter of the book you're reading, that's being lax. This initial concession will repeat

---

46. *The father of the modern Olympic Games.*

itself two, five, ten, a hundred times, and in the end, you'll spend at least two more weeks at sea. If I must get up ten minutes after lying down to change a sail because I feel my boat demands it, I don't hesitate for a second. And if I'm tired, so be it, I'll rest later.

Throughout the entire Golden Globe Race, even with my comfortable lead, I constantly fine-tuned every adjustment, checked that no seaweed had wrapped around my log or the rudder of the wind vane and had the sail perfectly matched to the wind's strength. Always with the same goal: to make progress as fast as possible towards my destination. I didn't expect such differences, but it's so easy, when sailing solo, to choose the path of least resistance, to cruise leisurely, to lower the spinnaker, to leave the boat to the wind vane. I once spent ten straight hours clinging to the helm in my cockpit just to squeeze out a few extra miles.

When sailing solo, you don't have anyone to 'shake you up', so you must be vigilant not to fall into a false rhythm. Sometimes, it requires a lot of willpower. Sometimes, you want to throw in the towel. It's no wonder the gaps were so significant in this race. The chosen boats were slow, complicated to manoeuvre and not originally designed for competition at all. These pitfalls sometimes result in dismal averages. Even more reason to constantly keep an eye on your competitors. I remember my friend Catherine Chabaud on her 60-foot yellow *Whirpool-Europe 2* during the 1998 Route du Rhum. We were battling for second place, and we had experienced a series of depressions. During the radio check-in, I heard her confess that she was exhausted, at her wits' end, ready to get a little sleep before putting up more sail. Naturally, that made me smile because I had already sent up all my sails to ensure she wouldn't catch up with me.

I admit to having a somewhat traditional view of racing boats. Maybe it comes from my age but I feel more in tune with monohulls with classic wooden or plywood interiors. I feel uncomfortable in machines made entirely of carbon, stripped to the extreme, making do with a beanbag that can be moved as the tack changes, a computer screen fixed to the bulkhead, a wireless keyboard and a tiny stove.

All my boats are similar, with a berth on each side in the main cabin, lee cloths preventing me from rolling off bunks, a nice chart table and a real galley.

During the Golden Globe Race, I mostly ate at the chart table or in the cockpit. The advantage when you're alone is that no one will comment if you decide to enjoy your meal in the buff and sit on the steps of the companionway.

Sometimes, I meet people who claim that I remind them of Éric Tabarly[47]. That's a misconception. The first time I encountered him was at his place on *Pen Duick* in the 1980s. While climbing aboard his boat, Tabarly accidentally let go of his sculling oar. Drifting with the current, it passed *Altair*, my ketch anchored nearby, and I picked it up. He came by promptly to retrieve it, and we exchanged a few words. Regardless of what people say, I've always felt closer to Bernard Moitessier's philosophy than Éric Tabarly's

---

47. *Tabarly was a French Navy officer and yachtsman. He developed a passion for offshore racing very early on and won several ocean races. (See page 181.)*

pragmatism. In my eyes, the latter was an innovator who took risks, while I tend to be more conservative and cautious. I've certainly read all Tabarly's writings, including his extraordinary victories in the English Transats of 1964 and 1976.

But unlike him, I've always set sail on relatively conservative boats. If someone had offered me a canting keel for the Vendée Globe or building a trimaran for the Route du Rhum, I would have said no. I'm too thoughtful, too rational and boats already cost enough without adding unnecessary risks to the ones that naturally come with them. Michel Adrien, who largely financed my massive namesake monohull for the Global Challenge – the wrong way round the world – was always more intrigued by the money I hadn't spent than by what I had spent. Even with a substantial budget, it never crossed my mind to overspend on non-essential things. Instead, I worked hard to afford my boats.

When I was a teacher, I had two separate budgets: One for the family and one for my personal boat. What I earned in sailing school, for instance, went straight into my boat fund. I worked at the Lorient fishing port for a long time while teaching. I did night shifts, during which I almost doubled my salary. Socially speaking, unloading tons of fish may not have been glamorous, but it was profitable.

I only had one fear: Being recognised. I was starting to become somewhat known in the world of offshore racing. It would have been enough for a guy or a parent of one of my students to identify me and I would have been in trouble.

For my fellow labourers, a 'sailor' could only be a well-off person always on vacation or a privileged daddy's boy. As for playing the role of a dockworker, I was fully committed, not pretending. The guys I worked with at the fishing port hadn't had much education, but that didn't bother me. I was on the same level as them, an 'occasional docker'.

The job was not only physical and required constant vigilance, but they also didn't cut you any slack. When you were assigned to the 'panel'[48], it was better not to mess up. There was several days' worth of fish at the bottom of the hold which smelled of warm diesel, and sometimes fish in an advanced state of decomposition, heading for animal feed.

From the deck, you had to guide the crane operator. A delicate operation. If one or two fish escaped from the bin and fell on the heads of the guys below, you would get a serious telling-off. I saw a dockworker going to hospital with a hook in his mouth and a drunken crane operator who had almost been lynched. They were tough guys.

These 'temporary' workers were on a list. If you were in the 100th position, you didn't have a job; if you were 75th, you did. At the beginning, you were at the bottom of the list, and then you moved up as people were fired or quit because the work was too tough. In the end, I was working two nights a week from midnight to 7am, sometimes even later – every Sunday and every Tuesday because I didn't have classes on Monday or Wednesday mornings.

---

48. *'Panel' refers to a hatch on the deck of a fishing vessel that provides access to the hold.*

Before heading to school, I would have a good shower and changed my profession. When I stopped to focus on offshore racing, my younger brother Philippe took my well-earned place on the list, no problem. He looked just like me and it went off without a hitch.

As a teacher, I 'fought' with my students to get them to write down the steps of their reasoning rather than rushing to try to do calculations in their heads. It's better to take your time and solve problems one by one, to go all the way, rather than rush and get it all wrong. When $2x = 3$, and x is $3/2$, there's no struggle. It's mathematics.

In any case, regardless of the subject, a teacher is an actor. He must not only interest his students, but seduce them, start again if things don't work out, redo them if necessary, and relax the atmosphere. You must be able to captivate them. That's certainly my showman side, but I love to have the audience in the palm of my hand, to move them like in a theatre or a concert. If you show any weakness, your students will exploit it immediately. This seductive side has always excited me, no matter the place or circumstance. I proudly embrace it.

It might sound conceited, but I love making people happy. It's in my nature. I don't think I have many enemies; I don't get into arguments with anyone, and that's a good thing because I hate that. I believe I am tolerant. In short, I think the world lacks tolerance.

During my first Vendée Globe, in addition to the accounts of my favourite sailors, I brought three books on board: the Bible, the Quran, and *Sea Birds*. I read the Bible and the Quran from cover to cover. The Quran was particularly interesting, because the translator had doubts and noted in the margins that he wasn't certain about the accuracy of his transcription compared to the original. He admitted that sometimes he interpreted and I liked that. I wanted to better understand this religion, and whenever the race left me with a bit of free time, I delved into a sura.

The Bible, on the other hand, was more familiar to me due to the countless hours of catechism I attended. It was given to me by my friend Eugène Dousal, a former archdeacon in Seine-Saint-Denis. I met him at the Lorient sailing school and did the infamous transatlantic delivery trip between Newport and Lorient, via Glénans, with him.

Over the years, he has christened all my racing boats, a ceremony to which I attach some importance. What Eugène says is always moving. He finds the right words, but has never tried to convert me or convince me otherwise. Perhaps I am too rational to believe in eternal life.

Supreme being or big bang, it is, in my opinion, man who is solely responsible for his destiny. I consider that we are simply 'passing through'. So, I take life as it comes, enjoy the moment, and congratulate myself on my ongoing projects. I live more in the present and the future than in the past. I have always had perspectives, desires and dreams. If they come true – and it often happens – great. If not, well, too bad, I move on to something else.

Chapter 17

My twelfth Cape Horn

GOLDEN°GL◑BE°RACE

On 10th November, after five exhausting days spent repairing my mast, I begin to steer a normal course, heading east-southeast. I haven't put my log back in the water, and I haven't known my precise position for several days. To make matters worse, with the low cloud cover, I can't even take a celestial sight. At my age, it's not the first time I've found myself in this situation. There's no need to panic or overthink it. The ideal route to Cape Horn is at 135 degrees, the wind is easing, and I can finally set more sail. I jot down, 'Come on, Jean-Luc, move your backside and climb up again!' I have to motivate myself as best I can; after all, this is the seventh time in just over four months that I've been forced into this dreadful exercise.

I can still hear myself telling Loïc Madeline, the editor-in-chief of sailing magazine, *Voiles et Voiliers*, who came on board a few weeks before the departure: "It's hard on a circumnavigation not to have to climb the mast at least once. I've prepared for the task but I have to admit I really don't like it." Case closed.

This time around, I spend another three hours up there. I manage, not without difficulty, to remove the pins from the turnbuckle at the end of the first spreader and then re-tighten it. Phew, I didn't play the monkey for nothing; the mast isn't too badly adjusted, and it seems to be holding up. My arms and legs are wobbly, and I've lost count of my aches and pains, but everything is okay. What worries me most since South Africa are the reinforcements supporting my spreaders, which have been squeaking incessantly when I'm on a downwind course. Over time, they have worn the mast, and I had to install some sort of tackle made of ropes to lock everything in place.

On 12th November, I cross another front. There are 35 knots of wind and horizontal rain. I seriously reduce sail but can't manage to alter my course. The steep sea and cross swell batter my boat, rolling it from one tack to the other, making life on board quite turbulent. I almost feel like I'm inside a punch bag. But what matters is that I'm back in the race. Finally, the sun returns. I'll take a nap at noon, reset my log and send my position as required by the rules.

I also decide to climb the mast once more to protect the rigging with some wide adhesive tape. I know all too well that in these waters, UV rays attack everything and eat away at the ropes. I'm keeping my fingers crossed that it holds up as long as possible.

Another gust of wind hits. The sea is truly dreadful, and the waves are treacherous and I wonder where they're coming from. *Matmut* is being assaulted from the side and from behind. Taking a sextant reading feels like a gymnastics challenge, especially since you must be at the top of a wave to see the horizon. Just going down into the cabin to get the instrument from its case and then bringing it back on deck is a feat. Since one of the two sextants is stuck due to salt, I have one fear: smashing the one that still works against the cabin or on a bulkhead and misaligning its mirrors.

As usual, when my batteries are well charged, I decide to raise my hydro generator which produces energy through the submerged propeller. Why didn't I think of it earlier? A particularly violent wave has literally torn off the rail and broken one of the two fittings that hold it attached to my stern. Already deprived of my solar panels, despite having two small emergency ones, I have no choice: I must make repairs at sea.

Here I am, lying down, contorted, in this precarious position that I detest. I inspect the damage and find that the broken fitting is the same one that allows me to adjust my two jibs (genoa and staysail). A replacement is necessary, at least in theory. The operation, of course, turns out to be much more complex. It's like trying to break down the wall of your kitchen to reach a faulty pipe without letting any plaster fall onto the floor. An operation that has to be carried out in the hostile environment of a moving boat and unpredictable weather.

I bless my two children, Élisabeth and Éric, for giving me a twelve-volt cordless Bosch drill for Christmas. I diligently drill my holes. Nuts, ball bearings, I must not forget anything. The ordeal is never-ending. After three hours, I give up and note: 'Tomorrow is another day. The wind has calmed down a bit, but not the sea. I don't dare speed up now. Better be careful.'

The next morning, I regain my composure and finally manage to repair that darn fitting. My hydro generator is operational again. My natural wisdom does not shield me from all the rookie mistakes. A breaking wave, a second of distraction and I take one of the protective bars of the sprayhood right in the face. In the mirror, the result is not a pretty sight. A boxer punched by a solid right hook wouldn't look much worse than me. According to my logbook, I take it rather philosophically: 'What a beautiful sunny day!' Proof that I've already moved on.

I try to dry what can be dried, especially my ski gloves, which I use when spending long hours at the helm. My ultimate luxury is to open a vacuum-sealed bag containing a new pair of underwear. I brought two sets of foul weather gear – bibs and jacket – that I use alternately, picking the drier of the two. However, I need to be careful not to get my boots too wet, as I only have one pair: Basic Guy Cotten boots at an unbeatable quality-to-price ratio.

I wanted to leave with Le Chameau boots with gaiters – the top-of-the-range boot used by all the competitors in the Volvo Ocean Race or the Vendée Globe – but they are not available in my shoe size. It's worth mentioning that with my small 47-48 size feet, my shoes are a little special. Even when ordered almost a year in advance, the manufacturer failed to deliver them.

I'm approaching the Horn (at 56 degrees south and 70 degrees west). The sea is churning under a series of violent squalls. Between the tip of South America and Antarctica, the Drake Passage generates a powerful swell that, coming from South Africa, Australia and New Zealand, encounters virtually no obstacle. In meteorological jargon, it's called the fetch. The waves have a gloomy hue that perfectly matches the Horn's jagged teeth. I'm running downwind with almost no sail, just a tiny bit of headsail up front. Roughly speaking, there are between 40 and 45 knots of wind, a swell I estimate to be between six and eight metres, with the occasional rogue wave exceeding ten metres.

I've just unrolled a tiny bit of the staysail, sheeted it in tight, and let the boat run. Since my passage in the 1992 Vendée Globe, I don't recall a Horn this challenging. Nevertheless, I've decided to get closer to the coast. In my damp blue notebook, as wet as a towel, I note: 'Watch out for the Ildefonso Islands.' These are a group of islands strung out in the Pacific almost due east of the Horn, and a potential obstacle when approaching the Horn from the northeast, the direction I was coming from. Fortunately, I have a highly precise electronic depth sounder that detects depths of over 300 metres, which is important when you don't have the reassuring position of GPS.

It's Friday, 23rd November, in the early hours of the morning. It's my twelfth Cape Horn rounding, the tenth one solo. I'm comfortably in the lead and feel a sense of liberation, difficult to describe, at the end of the endless 'Southern Ocean tunnel'. Tears well up in my eyes. Is it the wind or emotion, or perhaps the realisation that this is probably the last time I'll round it in a race? Certainly, it's a bit of all of them and a relief every time.

During my first Vendée Globe in 1989, I dreamt of sandwiches. Now, I'm content with a few slices of toasted bread and a good can of Hénaff pâté. That's enough to make me happy. While waiting for a beef stew to cook, my portion of Camembert cheese and some dried figs work perfectly fine. The seafood platter, the spider crab, the rare meat, soft-boiled eggs will have to wait. In the evening, to celebrate the occasion, I'll have a small terrine prepared by my mother-in- law, some calamari made by my friend from Noirmoutier, all accompanied by a perfect glass of red Bordeaux. I'm not complaining. I even brought along a can of corned beef signed by Robin Knox-Johnston to be opened only in case of an emergency. He, on the other hand, had taken 216 cans of corned beef and 244 of braised beef – just to mix it up.

It's been 145 days at sea. 50 years ago, to reach this same point, Robin Knox-Johnston took 86 days longer, and Armel Le Cléac'h during the last Vendée Globe in 2016 took 98 days less. I'm right in the middle, between the old and the new world. My impressions at Cape Horn are like a millefeuille, with a multitude of flavours and often very different tastes. I even approached it for real, on 1st January, 2014, during a cruise on *Le Boulard*, a kind of off-road vehicle for the sea designed to navigate these hostile areas. With Jean the skipper, Odile, my friends François and Gabrielle Marie, and their son Benoît, who had won the Mini Transat a few months earlier, we landed and spent the morning celebrating New Year with the lighthouse keeper, his wife and their son. That's how well I know the place.

There is a monument, erected 25 years ago by the Chilean navy, an assembly of five sturdy steel plates capable of withstanding gusts of over 100 knots, designed by Chilean sculptor, José Balcells Eyquem, that forms the silhouette of a seven-metre-tall albatross. It pays homage to sailors that perished attempting to round the Horn.

A rudimentary staircase carved into the storm-swept moorland allows access to it. For now, despite the mist obscuring all visibility, I decide to get as close as possible. I call Adan Otaiza, the lighthouse keeper, on the VHF. He responds immediately.

It must be said that in these parts, he probably isn't contacted by a sailing boat every day. We speak in Spanish. Since I know the house he is in, I feel like I'm there. I can clearly see that brick building with a red roof topped by the famous lighthouse, all attached to a small wooden chapel. Inside, it feels like a perfectly equipped vacation villa, like an Airbnb for a couple and two children. On the white walls, there are framed posters straight out of Ikea, and in the bedrooms, all the essential amenities: a sofa, television, internet router, and so on. The only notable absence: there's not a single neighbour in sight. The keeper – a Chilean navy serviceman – volunteers for a one-year stay. His supplies are delivered every quarter. There's no shortage of candidates and the work is quite reasonable: three daily weather reports, intermittent visual surveillance and a daily report.

While during the austral summer, from December to March, tourists are plentiful, for the rest of the year, visitors are scarce. Adan spots me approaching. He climbs to the top of the lighthouse, takes a photo of Matmut, a small piece of white sail barely distinguishable among the crests and, thanks to the marvels of modern technology, he posts it immediately on Facebook and Twitter. It's now my image's turn to go around the world.

I'm still under the staysail alone. The keeper wishes me fair winds, ending the 'nostalgia sequence'. It's high time to continue my long journey. A few hours later, waves break in front of me. Is it a rock or a shoal? Since I don't have a very precise map of the area, I bear away widely to avoid it. 'He who wants to live long as a sailor greets the squalls and rounds the points!' The last thing I need is to crash just a stone's throw from the Horn.

When you know nothing about the low latitudes and you're leaving them for the first time, you lose the fear that has been gnawing at your stomach since entering the Forties. But the feeling quickly returns when you go back there. The cold, the dampness, the solitude and the routine. The same actions, the same fatigue, the same apprehensions every day. On the chart, the crosses drawn in pencil don't advance, or if they do, it's painfully slow.

Of course, the light is fantastic, unique, and the prevailing wildness is both moving and challenging. But soon, anxiety takes over again, because of that barometer needle dropping and those long cirrus clouds piling up, not offering good omens. Only the albatrosses soaring above the crests seem eager for the storm's return.

The idea was nice to set sail 50 years later, exactly on the same date as Sir Robin Knox-Johnston. The problem is that being faster than him, I found myself in the south in the middle of winter, not the best time of year, to say the least.

The ideal time to pass Cape Horn is January, not

November. And the most surprising thing is that during my Atlantic crossing, I'll only have four days of summer. I'll cross the equator just before Christmas, and I'll be back in the middle of winter as I approach the European coasts. For the next edition of the Golden Globe Race in 2022, the organisers are going to delay their departure until September.

Finally, I point my bow northward. Reading zero degrees on the compass, I confess, for some time now, that's all I've been dreaming of. For a moment, I wonder about the opportunity to find a safe place to stop and check the condition of my damaged mast that obsesses me. But in the end, I decide to continue and take the shortest route between the coast and the Île des États (Isla de los Estados, or Staten Island). I cross my fingers. I still have 6,700 miles (over 12,000 kilometres) to go.

During my first Vendée Globe, at the same place, I rejoiced a bit too soon. Cape Horn is not Les Sables d'Olonne. Certainly, day after day, the sea gets calmer and the temperature rises. You feel better, you relax a bit. Your sleeping bag is almost welcoming, your sleep less disturbed. But the journey north is very long, and you are not entirely at ease. You are especially not safe from a nasty blow, the williwaws, those katabatic winds that descend from the Andean peaks and are of rare violence, sometimes worse than in the Indian or Pacific Ocean.

Chapter 18

Confessions & convictions, part 2

I'm not superstitious. I'm not the type to place a gold coin under the mast's foot, or to check that a canned terrine doesn't contain a long-eared animal. I have no issue with christening my boat on a Friday. I also welcome priests and girls on board, and I have no objection to changing the original name of a second-hand sailing boat. I even find it amusing that in the 21st century, there are still people who give credence to this array of eccentric beliefs. Without understanding their perspectives, I respect them. My son Eric, undoubtedly influenced by the 20 years he spent in the Navy, would never dare to utter the word 'rabbit' on a boat.

I may not be superstitious, but I am selfish. Nicole, my first wife, reproached me for it a lot. I think of myself first before thinking of others, that's obvious. Otherwise, I would have followed a different path to solo racing. Sailors are all inherently a bit egocentric. They share, they communicate, but from a distance. When I start a race, I feel no guilt towards those I leave on land. In fact, I am entirely focused on my goal: setting off, thinking of everything, not forgetting anything. So, I clear from my brain anything not directly related to my project. I love others, I respect them, but I can also, if necessary, put them in parentheses.

Knowing that I am surrounded by love, however, does me a lot of good. I remember my first Vendée Globe and the hours leading up to the start. For 20 years, no one had dared to compete in a solo, non-stop, unassisted race around the world. We really didn't know what we were getting into. My father, Roger, was probably putting on a brave face to hide his anxiety. My mother, Jacqueline, who was more reserved, wrote me a poem that I found both moving and realistic.

> *So what did they want*
> *These thirteen fearless men of the Globe?*
> *Travelling the harshest of seas*
> *Were they looking for happiness?*
> *Or to struggle?*
> *Or to suffer?*
> *Or to prove their worth?*
> *From sleeping countries, were they eager to leave?*
> *From a life too easy where comfort tires.*
> *Did they want the past to bring out fear,*
> *An ancient fear from deep within?*
> *Perhaps they felt that due to absence*
> *Their presence in our hearts would be more intense?*

If, at the moment of letting go of the last mooring line, you let too much emotion or stress show, you don't do your loved ones left ashore any favours. I was quite surprised, while walking on the pontoon at the start of the last Vendée

Globe, to see young sailors as white as sheets, overwhelmed by emotion. Their tears spread like wildfire to their loved ones to the point where leaving the channel turned into a real path of penance.

Personally, I'm always anxious when the adventure begins but also very happy to leave the pontoon. And it's this obvious joy that is most evident on my face. Does prioritising one's desires over everything else amount to a certain ingratitude? I don't believe so. My daughter Élisabeth, who works in retail, is a bit like me, totally involved in her professional life. She loves what she does and, naturally, her family life reflects that. Fortunately, she can rely more on her husband Karl's parents than on me.

Whilst I consider myself to be a decent family man, I must admit that I'm not very present for my grandchildren. When I'm not at sea, they occasionally come to Les Sables. Of course, I prioritise family gatherings. A few days after finishing the Golden Globe Race, I made it a point to catch up on all the birthdays I had missed.

Christmas matters to me too. For that occasion, I have fun on board sketching Christmas trees with their decorations, a nativity scene and baby Jesus in the middle. It's not very beautiful – barely better than my drawings in first grade – but it's the thought that counts. The 25th December, when you're at sea, is always a difficult time. You're alone, you know your whole family is gathered, and during that particular Golden Globe race, you didn't even have permission to make a phone call despite your satellite phone being within reach. To console myself, I planned a terrine (always prepared by my mother-in-law), a capon with chestnuts, a bit of foie gras and Camembert cheese, rhubarb, all accompanied by 'Ma Petite République', the organic wine from a Bordeaux producer, and a drop of rum. Marking the occasion in these circumstances is essential – at least for me. Solitude, competition, sport are among my primary concerns, but so is pleasure.

Some people sometimes describe me as ascetic. A journalist writing for *Libération* even imagined me in a monk's robe. Not true at all. As I mentioned, my father was a good pianist, particularly fond of jazz. I've inherited a bit of his joie de vivre, especially when it comes to music. I've enjoyed singing for a long time. While at boarding school, a blind teacher encouraged me in this direction. For him, I sang in churches and choirs. But soon, modern music replaced sacred melodies. I still have an impressive collection of 'live' albums from the greatest English bands of the 70s-80s. And at home, as the youngsters say, we always had 'a good sound system'.

My first 60-footer wasn't named *Éclipse* by chance. The nod to Pink Floyd is evident. Since my father worked at Europe 1 for a long time, I managed to get their address and, without too much hope, I boldly asked the members of the band to come and christen the boat. To my great surprise, a few weeks later, I received a very friendly response from Nick Mason, the drummer, who expressed his regret and apologised. On that date, he was on tour with Pink Floyd, but he wished me good luck with my voyage. Pink Floyd has always accompanied me on land and at sea.

In a different vein, I'm pleased that Hugues Aufray is *Adrien's* sponsor. We've become friends. He has even come to sing with my band, and one day, he invited me to join him on stage at the Zénith in Nantes. I was quite proud. Me joining the band we named 'Globalement Vôtre' (Overall Yours) was purely coincidental. At that time, in the 2000s, I sang here and there whenever I was invited, without any ambition. Two friends were celebrating their birthdays at the Petit Bar on the beach in Les Sables and had arranged for a band but they cancelled at the last minute. After various twists and turns, I found myself stepping in as a replacement with their friends whom I didn't know. We just had a phone call to get acquainted and discuss a few songs, nothing more.

The evening was a success, even though it was interrupted by the police called by the neighbours. A few performances later, Globalement Vôtre had its first real concert in front of the 600 guests of the Hénaff company celebrating its centenary. There are thousands of bands much better than us, but when it comes to creating a good atmosphere, we hold our own. We rehearse every Monday, unless I'm at sea. Our repertoire is well-known to all: Johnny Hallyday, Eddy Mitchell, Soldat Louis, Michel Sardou and Hugues Aufray, not to mention Pink Floyd … Informed music lovers may not necessarily share my musical choices and my joy of singing, but after all, what does it matter? Here again, I indulge myself and bring pleasure to others.

At the start and finish of my last circumnavigation, we didn't skimp on the festivities. Especially at the finish where I didn't expect to see Hugues, who was nevertheless there, on my boat, to sing his iconic 'Santiano' with me. I was over the moon. He's not really a sailor, but he composed a song especially for me: 'Aux vents solitaires' (To the Lonely Winds). At almost 90 years old, in a black leather jacket, jeans and black boots, accompanied by his young and pretty companion, he's an indefatigable troubadour who continues to tour France and the world. Next to him, I feel like a kid.

Speaking of kids, I genuinely worry about the younger generation. I find that there's a growing divide between those who work like crazy, study and pass extremely difficult exams, and the defeatists, the fatalists and those who say, 'Anyway, I won't find a job.' I'm not saying it was better before, but unquestionably, it seems that the share of leisure time is increasingly outweighing the hours of actual physical activity, and that's not necessarily good news.

Even though my nature still leans towards seeing my glass as half full rather than half empty, my optimism has been tested for some time now. Increasingly replacing humans with robots does not bode well. Unfortunately, as a teacher, I have seen too many children failing at school. Even in my time, vocational training like the CAP was considered a dead-end path, and it hasn't improved since. As a logical consequence, young people are arriving from all over Europe, and even farther afield, who will stop at nothing to take on even the most thankless jobs.

Add to that, intolerance, lack of respect and incivility, and the situation becomes even worse. An anecdote comes to mind. It was in 1986 when the Devaquet law, which aimed to reform the university system, was being protested by many. At that time, I was teaching at a private Catholic institution. One morning, students from the public high school next door arrived at our entrance shouting, "Saint-Jo, join us ... Devaquet, if you only knew!" They wanted to occupy our buildings. I stood at the school's entrance, intervened and didn't yield. They turned away while still chanting, "Saint-Jo, join us!" Today, I'm almost certain that if placed in the same situation, I would have been physically attacked or very close to it.

We communicate a lot through emails, and we have fewer face-to-face interaction. Email is convenient; it's fast, but sometimes dangerous because it's written too hastily. A simple phrase can fall flat or even offend someone. Face-to-face with your interlocutor, you observe their reaction, adapt and change your tone. In the end, this rush for speed, this constant immediacy, disturbs me. Since returning from my circumnavigation, I've hardly opened a book. I always have something more important to do. I've fallen into a hectic rhythm, and I'm a victim of a system that dictates its rules without truly consulting us.

At sea, despite the competition, the rivalry, you have time. Time to think and act. I agree, there are times when you need to react quickly, but you can also 'take a step back', think about the music you've listened to, meditate on the landscape you've admired. For seven months, I didn't follow the news. I didn't even feel the need to, whereas on land, I can't help but glance at the headlines flooding my smartphone.

If something very serious had happened, I suppose a ham radio operator would have alerted me. It's refreshing to disconnect a bit. Thanks to them, I followed the results of the World Cup in soccer and the positions in the Route du

Rhum, in which my friend Jean-Marie Patier participated on my nearly 30-year-old ex-red cigar boat. So upon my arrival, I didn't even know what a 'yellow vest' was.

Since I turned 21 – the legal voting age at the time – I've taken on my civic duty to the best of my ability. I didn't have any fixed ideas except one: never succumb to extremes. When I was younger, I didn't hesitate to support candidates who had no chance of winning but whose discourse was distinctive. Perhaps I've become wiser with age.

It must be said that it's increasingly difficult to separate the wheat from the chaff. Today, media and communication strategies often overshadow the actual policies. I don't mingle with politicians much. I know Catherine Chabaud, of course, who is now a Member of the European Parliament, and Annick Girardin. The latter, the current Minister of Overseas France, is the sponsor of my Rustler 36. She has been a good luck charm. François Mitterrand impressed me, if only because he managed to serve two consecutive terms. I have a very fond memory of the day he received the 13 competitors of the first Vendée Globe at the Élysée Palace, showing interest in each of us, even though he wasn't a sailor in the least. I believe I even wore a tie for the occasion. But even though, thanks to him, the VAT issues on our boats were resolved (the tax authorities then considered that participating in the Vendée Globe should be categorised as transport and therefore wouldn't allow us to reclaim VAT), I can't say I liked him much.

I've always had sympathy for Gilles de Robien, the former mayor of Amiens and minister. This politician seemed to me both moderate and honest. I hear a lot of people complaining about Emmanuel Macron. Frankly, would François Fillon, Benoît Hamon or others have done any better? In fact, I feel sorry for elected officials. They generate support and alliances, but they also attract a lot of hatred. A mayor, a deputy, a minister makes a decision that they believe is in the interest of the community, and instantly a significant portion of public opinion jumps on their case. Criticism is always easier than solving the problem.

You can call me a grumpy old man, but I feel much younger than the birth date that my ID card suggests. I receive a lot of letters from people of the same age as me, who tell me that they are motivated by my example. Being in your 70s is not a handicap. Proof of this is that you can even sail around the world at this age. Having the desire is fundamental.

If I have a message to convey, it's this. In the numerous talks I give everywhere, I don't say anything different, using simple words, and above all, my experiences to back it up. Organisers explain their issues to me, and I draw from my small arsenal of experience, and I adapt.

People first need to feel valued, to break out of the monotony of their daily lives. A few days after my arrival, I even received a call from the president of a national football club. His team, which had been doing well, was starting to lose game after game. He wanted me to try to boost the players' confidence and reverse the spiral of their failures. I'm naturally an optimist. Out of fatalism?

After six circumnavigations of the globe, I know that we can't fight against all the events and elements that come our way. There's nothing worse than a head-on collision. What we need to do is identify the problems, tackle them one by one, methodically assess their seriousness, and try – yes, try – to solve at least some of them. Once you reach that stage, anything is possible: a sequence of possibilities, luck adding to luck, a real inspiration. I believe in that.

Chapter 19

The endless ascent

GOLDEN°GLOBE°RACE

On 2nd December, 2018, I am sailing along the coast of South America. 'Heading 10 degrees, nice weather ... finally!' My school notebook is in a sorry state, swollen by the damp. I have opened a new one. The further north I sail, the more plastic bags and other debris I encounter. I learnt, thanks to the ham radio operators, that Uku Randmaa was also amazed to find so many things floating in the waters off South Africa. He even spotted a floating door. Every sailor's dread is to collide with a 'UFO', an 'Unidentified Floating Object'. On our vintage boats that don't exceed seven knots, it's certainly less problematic than on the fast multihulls that sail five times faster, but still, we're never entirely safe.

I have made a habit of listening to the hum of the hydro generator's propeller. I even know my exact speed based on the turbine's rotation. After a short nap, all I hear is the sound of water flowing along the hull and nothing else.

Naturally, I become concerned. Rightly so: The propeller is caught in an enormous fishing net that I've been dragging for several hours. The boat hook isn't enough and I have to grab a blade and painstakingly cut through the nylon mesh, one square at a time.

The next day, there's a change of scenery. 'Violent squalls of at least 50 knots. Under a single-reefed mainsail', my logbook notes. I did say that once past Cape Horn, we were far from out of trouble. The sun plays peek-a-boo with the low cloud and I have a hard time getting an accurate fix. It's not too serious: In the South Atlantic, the chances of encountering another boat are rare. I'll have to wait until I'm off the coast of Rio de Janeiro for a cargo ship to finally relay my position.

I had set out with two identical sextants – Freiberger sextants, true 'Rolls-Royces'. On a friend's suggestion, I named them 'Du' No. 1 and 'Du' No. 2 pronounced as 'Sextant-Du' (sounds like 'Sex-extended'). I admit it's somewhat risqué, but it amuses the audience – and some journalists. I'm grateful every day that I brought two because, in the middle of the journey, one of them suddenly jammed, probably due to the precipitation of salty air accumulating on the arc. This must have seized the rotation axis.

After the rain comes the sunshine. Here I am, becalmed, without a breath of air and an unbearable residual swell. The sails billow and collapse, flapping like ill-fitting shutters. I hate this, but don't get upset. What's the use? The rigging and my weakened mast are suffering, and so am I. To top it off, I must spend three hours at the helm with the engine running, with a new problem in mind: calculating the best performance-to-consumption ratio.

I have a depression far to the west in my sights, and to take advantage of the wind direction, I am forced to sail as close to the Brazilian coast as possible. At this rate, I'll end up at Copacabana. In fact, I can see the coast and it's high time to tack. Social media likes to mock: 'With his lead, VDH is making a detour to Rio and its lovely Brazilian girls in swimsuits ...' Yeah, right! It's the wind that forces me to tack. I'm now on a course perpendicular to the one that should take me to Les Sables-d'Olonne, and I'm starting to worry about a possible comeback by Mark Slats.

In the south, before my capsize, I had built up a substantial lead over him: Over 2,000 miles, at the very least, which is roughly half an ocean. Since then, he has been nibbling and nibbling away at my lead. As my logbook notes: '1/12/18: + 1,100 miles; 30/12/18: + 760 miles; 7/01/19: + 416 miles; in distance to the finish.'

I can't afford to relax, but the wind, once again, has disappeared. I pass the time trying to fish but with little success. Apart from a squid that jumped into the cockpit and ended up in the pan, I hooked a magnificent mahi-mahi that, for lack of a catch net, managed to slip away just inches from the transom. I only caught two or three flying fish, whereas during my previous circumnavigations and transatlantic races, I would find several of these odd flying creatures trapped under the sail bags, wings spread and mouths agape every morning.

Is this another sign of the poor state of our oceans?

I continue to cross through sargassum seaweed banks. I am amazed by their number and extent. It's the last day of the year. For my New Year's Eve celebration, I indulge in small pleasures: foie gras, wild boar stew and dehydrated strawberries in wine. And as one happiness never comes alone, Odile surprises me by participating in a radio communication session with a friend who is a ham radio operator near Nantes. Happy New Year!

I can't imagine for a moment that I could be overtaken by my Dutch rival. Nevertheless, I realise every day that he's a darn good sailor. So, I take the helm more and more to make the most of the slightest breath of wind.

On 6th January, I stay at the helm for eight uninterrupted hours – to cover 11 miles (20 kilometres) at the terrifying average speed of 1.37 knots (2.54 kilometres per hour). I also know that Mark, who doesn't have the same wind conditions, is moving significantly faster. How frustrating!

I patiently endure and listen to Philippe Labro's *L'Étudiant étranger* (*The Foreign Student*), which consists of six one-hour audio cassettes. At least that's something to pass the time. I need to stay focused and constantly adjust my sails, despite a breeze so weak that I can't even feel it on my skin.

It's also time to serve my penalty for calling Odile on the phone just after my capsize. The race organizers have imposed 18 hours of 'standing still' below the 20th parallel. I start by skirting this imaginary line, doing four hours to the east and four hours to the west in crosswinds. Without GPS, it requires a bit of skill, even for a former maths teacher. The Golden Globe Race 'police' have their eye on me. So much so that they believe I crossed the recommended line resulting in another warning and 3 more hours of 'standing still'.

After my penalty, the wind completely dies down. With

my fuel reserves exhausted, I have no choice but to endure this windless bubble in a high pressure system.

Certainly, this ascent up the Atlantic is becoming a real chore. My lead over Mark continues to shrink: 13/01/19: + 190 miles; 15/01/19: + 54 miles; 17/01/19: + 14 miles in distance to the finish. I can tell from the radio amateurs that those following my progress are getting worried. In hindsight, I'll even learn that some supporters were staying up at night to study the changing gaps and weather conditions.

I remain confident: I'm sailing much further north than my opponent, which means I'll reach the westerly winds before him. My mast groans under the onslaught of these short waves, typical when sailing close-hauled from the equator. Fortunately, I'm going to regain some distance on my pursuer. I keep an eye on him from afar, realising – thanks to the radio amateurs – that he's copying all my moves without exception, I tack and 'drag' him to the east, an area at the centre of the high-pressure system that I know is not very favourable. It's a cunning move frequently used in racing to control your opponent. Mine falls for it hook, line and sinker. My logbook triumphs: 'HE'S DEAD!' and the gap is widening this time in the right direction: + 101, +145, + 230, + 290, + 400 miles – the experience of competitions, which Mark may not have as much of.

There are now only five of us left in the race and, according to my calculations, I have only a few more days to go before reaching the finish line.

Mark Slats is now nearly 400 miles behind, Uku Randmaa and Istvan Kopar are still off the coast of South

America and Tapio Lehtinen is sailing in the Pacific. At this rate, the Finn will take at least three weeks longer than Robin Knox-Johnston, who, 50 years ago, returned to port after 313 days at sea.

Completely reassured, I decide to pass west of the Azores with the prospect of being carried by a good breeze to Les Sables d'Olonne. On Saturday, 26th January, Lionel, my faithful shore crew, along with Bob Escoffier and the photographer Jacques Vapillon, meet me 400 miles west of the finish line. It's nice to see familiar faces again. We chat over VHF radio and even in person for part of the morning, but as bad weather looms, they turn back in the early afternoon.

As soon as they leave me, the wind gradually picks up to 25, 35 and then 45 knots. I had hoped to be done with strong winds, weather vagaries and unstable situations. Just a few days ago, I was begging the wind gods for more wind, and now I have too much of it.

The swell rolling over the continental shelf, where the depths suddenly rise, is substantial. I'm not worried, but I don't forget that many sailors have experienced their worst gales while crossing the Gulf of Gascony – the 'Bay of Biscay', as it's marked on the nautical chart. Proof of this: while sitting at my chart table, I'm thrown as violently as during my capsize.

Despite having lost ten kilograms since then, the flight – over the steps leading down to the galley and the subsequent impact, are substantial. Result: The handrail near the stove is bent at 20 degrees, and the eight screws holding it in place have been torn out. The boat did indeed heel over, but fortunately, the masthead did not dip under the water.

I, who feared arriving close-hauled in cold, dry, easterly winds, am now content. I was very close to disaster, just 24 hours away from being truly freed.

Chapter 20

Victory!

GOLDEN°GLⵐBE°RACE

Despite the poor visibility, every 15 seconds, I see the three white flashes of the Armandèche lighthouse. It is the last major lighthouse built in France, 50 years ago. Then I can make out the one on the Barges, which, on its rocky plateau, marks the approach to Les Sables d'Olonne. It was the first lighthouse to be automated in 1971. Thanks to its 30,000 candelas of power, it reaches 13.5 nautical miles (25 kilometres). From the balcony of my apartment in Les Sables, every evening at dusk, I see all these beacons light up together, sweeping the horizon with their magical brushes. At the end of this circumnavigation, there is no need to check in the book of lighthouses if my identification is correct. I'm entering familiar territory.

My route marked on the paper chart from the Azores to Vendée is soaked like blotting paper. Every pencil stroke threatens to tear it apart. Tonight, I've been lingering a bit, aiming to cross the finish line around 9am, as the race committee requested. The sky is getting increasingly overcast, the sea is grey and the rain is starting to fall.

There's hardly more wind than when I started 211 days ago, but there's still that characteristic rolling swell.

I've used my last hours at sea to tidy up a bit on board. The photos of my loved ones, stuck here and there, have withstood the journey well, and the lithograph on the right in the cabin, a portrait of Joshua Slocum with his famous straw hat, hasn't budged. For seven months, the first solo circumnavigator in history has been keeping an eye on me.

It's time to close my final bag of trash. The race regulations are clear: all polluting waste must stay on board. Methodically, I've rinsed all my tin cans with seawater before placing them in double-lined, tightly sealed garbage bags. Upon my arrival, it's the race director, Don McIntyre himself, who must retrieve and weigh them. Roughly, I think it amounts to about 100 kilos. The scale will show 93, which is 13 kilos per month, 3.25 kilos per week, and 444 grams per day – still quite something.

Today, all long-distance sailors follow the same procedure. Regardless of the race, failing to bring your waste ashore can result in penalties. I remember during the first Vendée Globe Challenge, a competitor, to save weight, got rid of his spare mainsail and several autopilots, throwing them all into the sea. He didn't hide it. There's no doubt, mentalities have changed.

Since the toilets on my boat were sealed off, I made do with a basic bucket and my collection of *Le Canard enchaîné*[49] (after reading it). A minimal biodegradable sacrifice.

---

49. *Also called 'The Chained Paper', because canard is French slang meaning 'newspaper'. It is a satirical weekly newspaper in France.*

The day has dawned. I can now see the lampposts of La Chaume. My building to the left of the channel entrance overlooks the Priory of Saint-Nicolas. I've hoisted my large blue spinnaker to make better progress in this gentle wind. I don't even need to go down to the chart table to check the position of the finish line. It's also part of my daily routine. It's the South Nouch cardinal mark: A yellow and black buoy with two cones pointing downward and topped with a solar panel. A mark unlike any other, as it celebrates the conclusion of the Vendée Globe every four years and today welcomes the winner of the Golden Globe Race.

I've chosen to wear my navy blue Bermudes oilskin and its fluorescent yellow hood, still in perfect condition, and I'm savouring my last moments of solitude. I know that, in less than an hour, the contrast is likely to be stark. I've been waiting for this moment for many weeks. Am I euphoric? Let's say I feel a sense of excitement and great satisfaction. I set out for this: to arrive and, if possible, to win.

For someone who always calculates everything, I didn't even realise that by completing this adventure, I become the oldest winner of a round-the-world race in history. Robin Knox-Johnston informs me of this. He held the record: He was 67 years old when he completed the Velux 5 Oceans Race (formerly BOC) in 2006. What's more, as the winner of the 1968 edition, he pleasantly surprises me by being there amid a motley fleet that has come to meet me.

I don't know where to look anymore. Emotion is taking over. I try to respond to all the people calling out to me. Still, I remain focused because in front of all these spectators, I haven't installed the net that prevents the spinnaker from getting tangled around the stays. There's quite a bit of residual swell tossing my boat and I do want to avoid any incidents.

When I align myself with the Nouch and the grand jetty, I am across the finish line. It's an explosion of universal joy accompanied by a deafening concert of foghorns. I immediately lower my spinnaker. Odile and Lionel climb on board and bring me back to reality. They're all there, my children, grandchildren, my sisters, my brother and my friends. It's not a Vendée Globe arrival, but it feels like one.

The seawalls are submerged by a tide of umbrellas. The 1,600 metres of the channel, of which I know every stone, every arch, have never served as a better link between my passion for the sea and my life as a landlubber, which I must admit, satisfies me just as much.

As soon as the boat is at the quay, microphones are extended, and questions come pouring in. My excellent friends Hugues Aufray, Robin Knox-Johnston, Don McIntyre, Yannick Moreau, the newly elected mayor, come on board. It's thanks to the latter that the race started from here. When he was still a deputy, he had welcomed Don and us to the National Assembly to discuss the 2018 Golden Globe Race, and upon learning that English ports were reluctant to support this international event, he did everything, with the support of local sponsors, to ensure the race started from Les Sables-d'Olonne. Hats off to him!

Now, I must answer all the questions. I do so willingly, even if the exchanges inevitably turn to the same topics over and over. Of course, I am happy. Certainly, I missed my partner. What matters is the emotion, the empathy, the sharing that emanates from these precious moments. I sense a lot of sincerity all around, and that's what truly touches me, deep within. I open a magnum of champagne and, following tradition, generously sprinkle the crowd, take two or three sips, then share a few drops on the deck with my faithful boat, and with friends.

My entourage is concerned: Do my legs still work as they did seven months ago? I've never had seasickness, why would I have land sickness? Escorted like a rock star, I have 50 metres to cover to reach solid ground and reassure my loved ones.

I must submit to the ritual of the inevitable press conference – a delightful moment of narcissism – where I quickly return to my professorial habits. I don't withhold anything from my captive audience, not even the story of my twisted rail and my malfunctioning hydro generator.

There is Loïc Lepage, an unfortunate competitor who lost his boat, Patrice Carpentier and Alain Gautier, my comrades from the early days during the Vendée Globe 1989/90, Arnaud Boissières, Christine Briand, Jimmy Pahun, Catherine Chabaud, and, of course, Jean-Marie Patier, the man through whom it all began! Côme, their son, was allowed to skip school as it's not every day that you welcome your godfather back from the other side of the world. I'm on cloud nine. Lionel Régnier and a few buddies have gone out to secure the mooring lines for my Rustler 36 as a new storm is forecasted. My boat and I are safe, but I think of Mark Slats, my pursuer, who will surely have to endure it. We need to clear out before the tent sheltering us takes off. Obligations threaten my equilibrium just as much. Photos, protocols, podiums. Am I really myself? "What do you want?" Robin, who knows the drill, is being pragmatic. "A beer? A steak? A bath?" I mostly dream of a seafood platter.

In a small room at the fishing school, oysters, spider crabs and langoustines await me along with my loved ones. I savour this moment in every sense of the word. Then the interviews resume, with the same old questions. What makes this moment so special? Impressions, questions and comments fly in all directions. Naturally, the situation is exaggerated. They talk to me about being an example for young people searching for meaning but also a role model for seniors in search of hope. The great unifier of schools and nursing homes! It all seems a bit surreal to me but I accept the excitement; it's part of the deal and it makes me happy, but it really needs to calm down a bit too.

The wind is gradually picking up, getting stronger and reaching 60 knots, uprooting some trees near Port Olona. This adds excitement during the interviews I'm forced to do on board the boat, which sways in all directions under the gusts. A young reporter is on the verge of nausea. Odile and my friends have prepared a small gathering for me in the evening (still 130 guests!) with my full music band and my friend Éric Bolo and, of course, Hugues Aufray. In the middle of the night, the guests seem more tired than me. I rediscover life of a 'normal' person, with its simple pleasures and harmless distractions.

In the days that follow, the press praises me. My inbox is overflowing. Even *Paris-Match* sent two of its reporters and, 50 years after Moitessier, dedicated six pages to my adventure. My neighbours in Les Sables-d'Olonne, mostly retirees, have signed a poster that hangs in the entrance of my building. The attention touches me as much as all their little notes, these signs of admiration that accumulate day after day.

I, of course, attend the arrival of all my competitors. Mark, who negotiated the final storm well, and Uku, who happily reunites with his young wife and his baby twins, Istvan, overjoyed, who, as a conclusion, climbs his mast in the channel. Every time, day or night, the people of Les Sables are there, warm and supportive.

Easter Monday, 50 years to the day after Robin Knox-Johnston's arrival and its summer in Les Sables for the prize-giving, especially mine, £5,000 just like 50 years ago, except that back then, you could buy a little house with that amount.

All the competitors have come back from all corners of the planet to celebrate this. I'm touched. Well, almost all. Two are missing: the Finnish sailor Tapio Lehtinen, still at sea in the doldrums, who will arrive in mid-May in Les Sables with his hull covered in goose barnacles, and the Australian Kevin Farebrother, conquering Everest for the fourth time.

This prize-giving ceremony touches me deeply. Not only do I reach the highest step of the podium for the first time after a circumnavigation, but I also have the chance to host the party myself with my band and my musician friends, Bruno, François, Michel, Pierre Laurent and even Hugues Aufray, who is touring in the East of France, is part of it.

Éric Bolo, who has been with me for all my departures, and Michel Devillers, who competed in the Mini-Transat like me, join us on stage. 2,000 people have made the journey. I couldn't have dreamed of a better welcome and a more beautiful celebration.

Chapter 21

And now

This time, I believe I have reached the 'legal' retirement age. *At least when it comes to solo races around the world.* I emphasise the phrase because every word in it matters. In hindsight, I wouldn't want anyone to say that I didn't keep my promises. I will not defend my 'title' in the next edition of the Golden Globe Race in 2022. If you have read my account carefully, you will understand the reasons for this decision. Of course, I'm not immune to distant horizons. I long to be at sea. I can marvel at the unique geyser of a whale passing near my boat. But I'm not strictly a romantic. I'm a pragmatist.

Due to its overall pace and the slowness of the boats used in the Golden Globe Race, it could have turned it into a meditation session for me. However, that wasn't the case. My natural inclination as a racer and competitor always prevailed. Am I too down-to-earth, some might say superficial? That doesn't bother me. I've never claimed to be a philosopher.

For 40 years, I've been content with adding up races and adventures, and that suits me just fine. My track record is what it is, but I'm fully satisfied with it. I finished fourth in the first Mini Transat in 1977 and the Route du Café in1993, second in the Mini Transat in 1979 and the BOC Challenge in 1986, and second in the Route du Rhum in 1998. I came in third in the first Vendée Globe in 1990. I was the IMOCA world champion in the period 1992-1996, thanks in part to my second place finish in the Vendée Globe in 1992 and my third place finish in the BOC Challenge in 1994. I've held the record for circumnavigating the world the wrong way – meaning against the wind and currents – in 122 days, since 2004. It's the last and only record held by a monohull around the world. In the end, I won my sixth and final round-the-world race in January 2019. I've always sailed on simple, economical and reasonable sailboats.

I've rounded Cape Horn 12 times and crossed the equator 17 times. As someone who appreciates numbers, I've never precisely calculated the number of nautical miles I've accumulated in racing, sailing schools, cruising, deliveries and racing, but it must exceed 250,000, which is approximately 463,000 kilometres, nearly ten laps around the planet in total.

I remember as if it were yesterday when my son Éric, seven years old at the time, angrily kicked the car tyres as I left home for my second Mini Transat. Seeing his father leave again had more than irritated him, and at the time, I didn't fully grasp the extent of his frustration. That was exactly four decades ago. Like father, like son. Éric, in turn, spent many years travelling the world's seas, not by sail but aboard naval vessels, and he, too, received some dismayed remarks from his loved ones. Today, he still works for the French Navy as a reservist and oversees all things related to sailing at the Naval Academy. My daughter Élisabeth owns a sailing yacht and dreams of crossing the Atlantic with her husband. I would find it very difficult to dissuade her.

I've heard that I may take on future responsibilities in the organisation, even becoming the race director of the Golden Globe Race. Nothing is certain yet, but I'll consider it when the time comes. It's nothing more than a 'dockside rumour', as they say in the industry. If asked for my opinion, of course, I'll provide my input, but it will be limited to that. My friend Don McIntyre has done an excellent job, and it's only fitting that he continues. The price of success: around 20 competitors have already pre-registered for the next edition in 2022.

There are multiple reasons for my victory. Firstly, I believe I had the best-prepared boat. I relied on highly committed support team. Thanks to *MATMUT* and Armor Lux, my budget was comfortable without being extravagant. It's evident that my five previous circumnavigations greatly contributed to optimising my approach to the race and the overall management of the boat. For example, I always made sure to maintain a good level of hygiene on board, anticipating approaching storms to seize the opportunity for a shower and tending to any injuries as soon as they appeared. When sailing solo, it's tempting to let oneself go or even become 'ragged'. The opposite is what one should strive for and never forget that 'experience is a lantern that you carry on your back and it only illuminates the path that you've travelled.'

Such an endurance race is also won in the preparation. The better you prepare, the less you expose yourself to technical issues. It's undoubtedly no coincidence that Mark Slats and Uku Randmaa, respectively second and third[50], had both already completed a previous circumnavigation. Even though the race was tough (seven retirements, five capsizes, only five finishers out of 17), but unlike the 1968/69 race, there were no fatalities.

Throughout this circumnavigation, I systematically thought and visualised my manoeuvres in my mind before executing them. It's somewhat like the training sessions I impose on inexperienced crew members when I take them on for a regatta. When sailing solo, you have plenty of time, so you might as well make the most of it. There's never any use in getting flustered or rushing. Hot-headed skippers who 'lose their cool' at the slightest provocation have no place on board. Sailing requires calm, wisdom and humility.

I think back to Alain Gerbault. He weathered storm after storm, even in the trade winds. When I was young, I took such stories at face value. When sailing solo, it's always easy to go beyond the limits, engage in one-upmanship, or dramatise a situation.

Occasionally, I encounter pleasure sailors who use exaggerated language to describe their experiences, where they allegedly sailed in 50 knots of wind or even more. No one goes out in such wind. What's the point of exaggerating? The sea deserves more than fabrication; it deserves respect.

---

50. *Final ranking of the Golden Globe Race 2018: 1. J.-L. Van Den Heede (France), 2. M. Slats (Netherlands), 3. U. Randmaa (Estonia), 4. I. Kopar (United States), 5. T. Lehtinen (Finland).*

I'm certain that my mathematical background also contributed to my success. All in all, especially over such a long period, rationality and precision are two virtues that are welcome on board. I have no intention of excluding sailors with a literary or poetic inclination, but the fact is that the current trend in competition favours scientists more readily.

The best modern sailors, like Franck Cammas, François Gabart, Thomas Coville, Armel Le Cléac'h, Benoît Marie, Yoann Richomme, Sébastien Simon – who could all be my sons – are pure mathematicians when they are not engineers in the truest sense of the word. The records and performances achieved in recent years are directly dependent on their skills and their vision of the future. It's the nature of humanity to always strive further, higher and faster. However, behind all these new technologies, the human element must always take priority.

I've sold my faithful Rustler 36 to a New Zealand sailor who is already registered for the next edition of the Golden Globe Race, and who specially came from the land of the long white cloud to complete the transaction.[51]

I knew I wouldn't last long without a boat, and that enjoying 'OPB' (other people's boats) only lasts for a while. After a week of vacation spent cycling around the Luberon with an electric bike, I acquired my 20th boat, an 11.35-metre X-37 racing-cruiser made in Denmark, much

---

51. The buyer of the boat was New Zealand sailor, Graham Dalton. He was disqualified from starting the 2022 Race, because he failed a required medical examination.

more modern and faster than *Matmut*. With my latest toy, named *Matmut II*, I'll race with my friends, occasionally sail with my family and continue to apply the principles I share in my lectures: find pleasure, push your limits, manage the unexpected as best as possible, and always stay optimistic.

Acknowledgements

I was able to participate in the Golden Globe Race thanks to MATMUT, which has been effectively supporting me since the beginning of 2016 and a loyal partner who will continue to support me for the regattas of 2020. I also had a small partnership with Armor Lux / Bermudes, which was already present for my circumnavigation the 'wrong way' around the world and will also continue to follow me in 2020.

Many other companies have helped me technically to the best of their abilities: Acuitis, Akena, Ciel et Marine, Cotten, Cousin Trestec, Facnor, Formacoupe, Gréement Import, Hénaff, Honda, Landreau, NV Equipment, Plastimo, Super U La Chaume, Shom, Sparcraft, Templi Cuir, Voilerie Tarot, Volvo Penta, Yacht Care.

I also thank all the friends who generously gave their time: Eugène Doussal, Michel Devillers, Gisèle Taelemans, Jean Billet, Gilles Cosson, Jean-Marc Arthot, Patrick Barrett, André Geffard, Soizic Dary, Jason, Odile and Françoise Lange, Jean-Louis Leclerc, Guy Roger, Alain Zimeray, Jean-Michel Bernard and his winemaker friends from Bordeaux, not forgetting all the radio amateurs who followed me diligently, members of the Vogue Mini association, my crewmates, my Globalement Vôtre group, as well as Hugues Aufray and Éric Bolo.

Matmut was perfectly prepared for this competition thanks to Lionel Régnier, Olivier Morice and Antoine Delhumeau, not to mention Port Olona.

Lastly, I thank Don and Jane McIntyre who created and led this adventure masterfully with their team in partnership with Yannick Moreau, president of the Sables d'Olonne agglomeration, whose energy and passion for sailing were the driving force behind this event.

And if you enjoyed this book, it's thanks to Didier Ravon, Benoît Heimermann and the teams at Stock whom I thank.

Plate section photographs:
Pages 1-3 © Van Den Heede family archive
Pages 4-5 © Fernhurst Books Limited
Page 6 © Jean-Luc Van Den Heede
Pages 7-8 © Christophe Favreau / GGR / PPL

Making Waves

The real lives of sporting heroes on, in & under the water

A sneak preview about another French sailing great from another book in the Making Waves series:

Last Voyages
by Nicholas Gray

10
The Life and Last Voyage of Eric Tabarly on board his Yacht *Pen Duick* (1998)

In June 1962 Eric read about a British organised single-handed Transatlantic race, which had become known as the OSTAR, the second running of which was to start from Plymouth on 23 May 1964. The first race had been held in 1960 with five entrants and had been won by Francis Chichester in this boat *Gipsy Moth III*. Tabarly became determined to enter the 1964 race and win it. He just needed to decide on what boat to take. The old *Pen Duick*, with her heavy gaff rig, was not suitable and Eric headed to Brittany to talk to his old friend Gilles Costantini about the possibility of building a new yacht designed specifically for the race.

Gilles and his brother agreed to build one at their own expense, which they would lend to Eric for the race. Work began in October 1962 on a light displacement 10 metre yacht to be called *Margilic V*. She was launched in April 1963 and Eric took her on several offshore races. Eric soon realised that he could easily manage a much larger (and thereby faster) boat and persuaded the Costantinis that what he really needed for the OSTAR was a bigger and stronger one. After much discussion, plans were drawn up for a longer version. She was to be built out of plywood with a multi-chined hull and a long counter. She was to be ketch rigged to keep all sails a manageable size. Tabarly did not have any money to pay for such a boat but the Costantinis again came to his rescue. They agreed to sell *Margilic V* and put the proceeds toward the cost of this new one. Eric was to find the rest of the money, when he could.

Work started in January 1964, only five months before the start of the race. The boat was 13.60 metres long (44 feet), with a draught of 2.20 metres and a beam of 3.40 metres. She was launched on 5 April and the bare hull taken to the French Naval shipyard at Lorient, where the French Navy had agreed to finish her off. The work was completed and she was officially named on 9 May 1964 as *Pen Duick II*. There was barely time to rig and fit the sails and mount the self-steering gear before Tabarly had to leave for Plymouth, which he did on 16 May.

Tabarly arrived at Millbay Dock in Plymouth two days later and immediately began to assess his rivals. The first he observed was Francis Chichester, who was sailing the race again in his faithful *Gipsy Moth III*. Most of the other entries were heavy conventional cruising boats, seaworthy and slow but able to cope with heavy weather. There was a smattering of multihulls and, of course, Blondie Hasler, the originator of the race, in his junk rigged Folkboat *Jester*.

The other competitors were intrigued by *Pen Duick II*, many wondering whether she was too light, too fragile and too big for one man to handle. Tabarly for his part was determined to beat Britain at her own game.

Before the start it soon became clear that the race was really to be a needle match between Chichester and Tabarly, between England and France. Chichester, attired as ever in double breasted navy blazer and club tie, was a picture of calm and good organisation against the young quietly-spoken Breton naval officer frantically trying to get his steed ready as the last pieces of equipment were fitted and made to work.

After a poor start Tabarly soon overtook Chichester and led a procession down the English Channel to the open Atlantic. The weather threw up the usual brew of westerly gales, followed by periods of light winds with fog but, along with these, there was a fair share of favourable easterly winds. Tabarly experienced a series of problems but kept the boat sailing fast. First his self-steering gear gave up but he soon learnt how to trim the sails to keep *Pen Duick II* on course. He spent long hours at the helm, getting little sleep. Then his halyards at the masthead came adrift requiring him to climb the mast, a perilous thing to do when alone on a boat pitching and rolling in an Atlantic swell.

Tabarly arrived at the finish line by the Nantucket lightship at 10.45 on the morning of 18 June, in a time of 27 days and 4 hours. Chichester arrived two days later, having taken 29 days, compared to the 40 days he took in the first race. On his arrival Chichester gave Tabarly a warm handshake and said, "It is an honour to have been beaten by a sailor such as you."

The whole of France went wild for Tabarly. Not only had a Frenchman beaten the English, but they now had a new hero in this 32-year-old naval officer. 'A Breton now rules the waves', as one newspaper put it. In entering this race Tabarly had only two ambitions – to cross the Atlantic single-handed and to beat the English. He had achieved both.

After the race Tabarly was taken to Washington where the French Ambassador presented him with the Legion d'Honneur, France's top award. Eric then sailed *Pen Duick II* to New York where the boat was loaded onto a cargo ship for a free trip back to France. Tabarly was given free passage home on the liner *France*.

🪶FERNHURST│BOOKS

Find out more at **www.fernhurstbooks.com**

Making Waves

The real lives of sporting heroes on, in & under the water

A sneak preview of another circumnavigation that features in the Making Waves series:

The First Indian
by Dilip Donde

1
A Path Less Travelled

"Dilip, are you in some sort of trouble with the Navy?" asked my mother one evening as we finished dinner at home in Port Blair. I had pushed away the empty dinner plate absentmindedly and was back to working on my laptop.

"What makes you think so?" I asked, trying to sound as nonchalant as possible while my brain was busy trying to word a suitable reply. The moment I had been apprehensive about for the past two months seemed to have arrived.

"Why have you suddenly started getting so many calls from Naval Headquarters, including the office of the Naval Chief? I think it is all very unusual so will you please tell me?" She had been staying with me for the past nine years and must have noticed the change in my routine since I got back from a sailing trip to Mumbai two months back. Through the years I had made it a point never to take any work home, howsoever busy the schedule. Since my return, however, I had been sitting almost every evening with a laptop borrowed from the office, reading up and writing well past midnight.

"I won't call it trouble but, yes, there is something I got myself into when I visited Mumbai for the sailing trip. I didn't tell you earlier as the whole thing still appears a bit harebrained and unrealistic to me," I mumbled, trying to find the right words to break the news and minimize any possible resistance.

"You can tell me whatever it is," persisted my mother.

"The Navy has been looking for someone to undertake a solo circumnavigation in a sailboat and I volunteered, though I am not exactly sure what it involves." I decided to play it straight, acutely aware of my terrible diplomatic skills, and waited for her reaction. The reaction was surprisingly positive, though not too unexpected.

"That is very good. Give it your best shot, opportunities like this don't come every day, but remember it is a one-way street!" she responded after a pause. "Don't ever think of backing out."

I decided to test her further by telling her that there was a good possibility that I may not come back alive from the trip. No Indian had undertaken such a trip, less than 200 in the world had been successful, and no one kept count of the unsuccessful attempts. That didn't deter her much as she calmly replied that I had to go some day like everyone else and it would be far better if I went trying to do something worthwhile! All she asked, in return of her full support, was to be able to read up as much as she could on the subject.

With her full support assured, I decided to fill her in on the events so far....

On 27 Apr 2006, before the start of the Mumbai to Kochi J 24 sailing rally that I was participating in, I met Capt Dhankhar, the Navy's Principal Director of Sports and Adventure Activities. Since he had flown down to flag off the rally along with the Chief of the Naval Staff, or CNS, the conversation was about ocean sailing in the Navy. As I escorted him to the Sailing Club moorings, he almost casually mentioned that the Navy was toying with the idea of sponsoring a solo circumnavigation by a naval officer.

"Can I be a part of it in some way?" I blurted out, stopping him in midsentence, throwing naval protocol to the winds. I just couldn't help it, the whole idea sounded so exciting though I had no clue what exactly was involved.

"Would you like to take it on? Should I tell the CNS that you have volunteered or do you need a little time to think about it?" he asked in his characteristic measured tone, with a hint of scepticism.

"Yes sir, please do tell the CNS that I want to volunteer, I don't need any time to think!" I replied, my brain in overdrive. Less than a minute back I was ready to play any part, howsoever small, in

this unknown project because it sounded interesting and suddenly the entire project seemed to be falling in my lap. I didn't bother to ask what exactly the Navy had in mind, all my fuzzy brain could sense was that this was something exciting and I shouldn't let go of the opportunity.

"Okay, now that you have volunteered, can you make a project report and send it to me by next month?"

In less than five minutes of what seemed like casual talk, I had gotten myself into the biggest soup in my life with a very vague idea about what exactly it was!

The Captain had been my instructor during my Clearance Diving course and had observed me closely during those stressful days. That, along with my declared enthusiasm for ocean sailing and my past experience as the Executive Officer of INS Tarangini during her first round the world voyage in 2002-2003, probably prompted him to check if I was interested in this project. Apparently I wasn't the first person he had asked but was definitely the first to fall for the idea, thus ending his search.

Later in the day, the CNS, Adm Arun Prakash, flagged off the rally. In his speech he declared that the Navy was ready to sponsor a solo circumnavigation under sail provided someone volunteered to take on the challenge. As we lined up for a group photograph, he approached and said, "Dilip, I heard you have volunteered!" I just nodded my head and murmured, " Yes sir. Let us see."

"So that is the story so far. Now I am required to make a detailed project report and send it to Naval Headquarters as of last month, which explains the frequent calls from Delhi. Honestly, I don't have a clue about the subject and have been trying to read about it on the Internet, which seems to be the only source of information here." I promised my mother that I would pass on whatever I read on the subject to her and got back to finalizing my report. Her unstinting support was a burden off my head. I didn't realize it then, but I had just conscripted the first member of the team for 'Sagar Parikrama', as the project would be called.

More than a month went by and I still hadn't submitted my project report. One reason was a fairly busy work schedule that allowed me to read up on the subject only after dinner at home; the other, a total lack of knowledge about the subject. It would be an understatement to say that I was groping in the dark. The more I started reading, the more I started realizing that this was not something romantic and poetic as I had initially thought but would involve a lot of hard work and would be far more difficult than what I had imagined. Surprisingly, though, that increased my excitement and determination to make it happen.

By Jul 2006, I managed to submit my project report to Naval Headquarters (NHQ) and decided that if I had to do a circumnavigation it had to be a proper circumnavigation under sail, going through the Southern Ocean, round the three Great Capes, Cape Leeuwin, Cape Horn and the Cape of Good Hope. I could have proposed following the route taken by the previous Indian sailing expeditions in *Trishna*, *Samudra* and INS *Tarangini* through the Suez and Panama canals, called it a circumnavigation and no one would have been wiser, in the country at least! In fact, on hindsight, things would have turned out to be much simpler as I could always have pointed at 'precedence', something that opens many a door when dealing with the bureaucracy. I could have had a whale of a time stopping at 40 to 50 ports over a period of a year or two with a smooth sail through the Trade Winds! But then that wouldn't have been the real thing. Even if the Navy, and the taxpayer who was essentially funding my trip, didn't realize it, I would, and it just would not be right!

FERNHURST|BOOKS

Find out more at **www.fernhurstbooks.com**